THEN AND THERE SERIES
GENERAL EDITOR
MARJORIE REEVES, M.A., PH.D.

D0927373

Cortes and the Aztecs

JANE DORNER

Illustrated from contemporary sources

12735-46

LONGMAN

LONGMAN GROUP LTD
London

*Associated companies branches and representatives
throughout the world*

© Longman Group Ltd 1972

*All rights reserved. No part of this publication
may be reproduced, stored in a retrieval system,
or transmitted in any form or by any means,
electronic, mechanical, photocopying, recording,
or otherwise, without the prior permission of the
Copyright owner.*

First published 1972
Sixth impression 1980

ISBN 0 582 20529 8

*Photoset in Malta by St. Paul's Press Ltd
Printed in Hong Kong by Wing Tai Cheung Printing Co Ltd*

Contents

To the Reader

We have grown so accustomed to seeing pictures of astronauts in space that we tend to forget the tremendous amount of calculation that goes into planning every minute of a space explorer's day. We forget, too, that explorers did not always have the benefit of modern technology to guide their movements.

In the sixteenth century an explorer was very much on his own. Once he had set out with his ships and crew, nobody could keep track of his journey. Nor did he know exactly where he was going himself. He just had to rely on the sailors' skill and the few instruments they had to keep them safe. Maps were inaccurate and the explorers had to chart the way as they went.

It is not surprising that when they sighted land, they were overwhelmed by the discovery. They felt they had a great deal to bring to the new land and the desire to conquer it was very strong. The men who went to America were called 'conquistadors' which is a Spanish word meaning 'conqueror'. They were men of exceptional daring and lived in conditions of great physical hardship. One of these men was Hernan Cortes, who set out in 1519 with a small Spanish force to conquer Mexico.

This book is the story of the conquest. It is about a man who was mistaken for a god, who took a mighty emperor as his prisoner, and gained a great treasure of priceless golden jewellery and precious objects. It tells of a group of men who saw the strange customs of another people, and were forced to destroy them.

HOW TO PRONOUNCE MEXICAN NAMES

Most Mexican names are in Nahuatl, the language of the Aztecs. They are difficult to pronounce because of the sound 'tl' which is at the end or beginning of most words. It is pronounced like the 'tl' sound in the word 'settle'. The letter 'z' is usually pronounced like an 's'. If you don't know how a word should be pronounced, look it up in the Glossary, where Mexican words are listed separately, with the pronunciation in brackets.

4

1 Who Were the Conquistadors?

It all began with Christopher Columbus – and he never really meant to become a conquistador. Columbus set out to find a sea route to the east so that the merchants of Europe would be able to bring back spices, rich silks, fine cloths, dyes, ivory, diamonds and all kinds of beautiful things, without making the tiring journey overland. In the fifteenth century this was a very dangerous expedition. All the major European countries were anxious to find a sea route because trading with China and Japan and especially the Spice Islands in the East Indies had become very important.

But everyone thought Columbus's idea was quite crazy. He was saying that there was another way to get to the East Indies – not to sail east and follow the same direction as the overland *camel trains**, but to go west and sail round the world. He thought the journey would only take three weeks, and tried to persuade the King of Portugal – the country Columbus had made his home – to give him money for ships and a crew. But the King of Portugal would not listen to his idea. Even Columbus's arguments that Portugal was probably only half way round the world did not convince the King. Nevertheless Columbus was determined to put his idea into action and finally he persuaded Ferdinand and Isabella of Spain to fit out an expedition for him. They didn't quite believe Columbus could do it, but they were willing to let him try and, on 3 August 1492, he set sail with his three ships, the Niña, the Pinta and the Santa Maria.

It was not so easy to persuade sailors to come with him because, of course, they risked their lives. There is a story that he

---

*All words printed in *italics* in the text are explained in the Glossary.

Columbus's flag ship The Santa Maria

made the sailors play a game of dice with him. If they won, they could choose to stay at home, but if they lost, they had to come on the voyage. Life was very hard on the ships. Only the officers had bunks to sleep in; the others slept in their clothes on the deck. They ate salt pork, dry *cassava bread* and fish. The voyage took much longer than the three weeks Columbus had allowed, as the expedition had to stop while one of the ships was repaired in the Canary Islands. They set sail again and, after a month, supplies were getting low, and they still had not seen land. Many sailors who did not believe in Columbus's idea, thought they should turn back before they were completely lost in the Ocean, but Columbus persuaded them to give him three more days. On the third day, 11 October, they saw land.

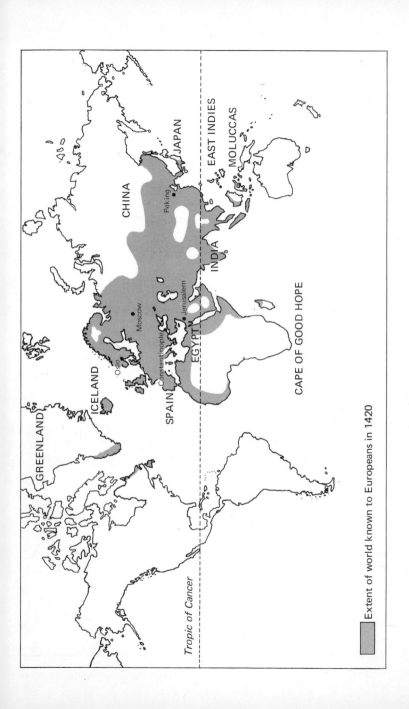

GREENLAND

ICELAND

Oslo

SPAIN

Constantinople

EGYPT

Moscow

Jerusalem

INDIA

CHINA

Peking

JAPAN

EAST INDIES

MOLUCCAS

CAPE OF GOOD HOPE

Tropic of Cancer

Extent of world known to Europeans in 1420

Only it wasn't the East Indies!

As an idea there was nothing wrong with Columbus's plan to sail from Portugal to the east – except that his calculations of time and distance were wrong. But, in fact, there was something Columbus could not have allowed for because he did not know of its existence. He did not know that the continent of America lay straight in his path.

The map on p. 7 shows the extent of the known world in Columbus's day. The shaded areas show the lands that were marked on the maps of the day. It was inevitable that Columbus's party would land somewhere on America and not surpris-

Columbus sails to America

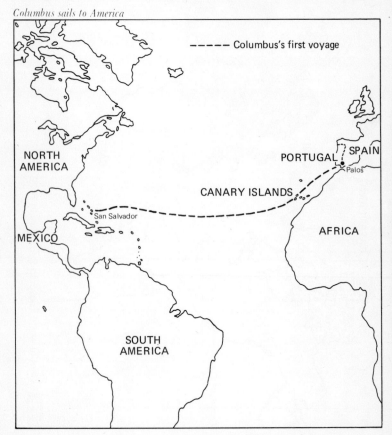

ing that they should think at first they had reached the east. They had been sailing quite long enough and, when they saw the dark skinned people who lived on the island where they landed, they thought they looked very much like Indians. Men and women went naked and had dark skins and long, straight, black hair. Columbus obviously thought it was an island off the mainland of Japan and, on learning that there were many more islands, he called them the Indies. Later, when it was discovered that the islands were not the East Indies, they were called the West Indies because they were on the western route to the east.

Columbus and his men had come to trade, so they explored the island and its people and found them easy to trade with. Columbus wrote of them: 'They have no iron or steel or weapons. They are so *guileless* and generous with all they possess that no one would believe it who had not seen it.' The explorers exchanged their red caps, glass beads, hawk's bells and tambourines for golden jewellery, parrots' feathers and balls of cotton.

It looked as if trade with the newly discovered people might be as profitable as the old trade routes. Orders came back from Spain that they were to found a settlement on the island, and so the first Spanish colony in the Americas was formed. This was the island of *Hispaniola*, now Santo Domingo and Haiti. Columbus, therefore, became the first conquistador.

He never really understood the importance of his discovery and did not realise that the riches of the new land would be far more important than the advantages gained from finding a trade route to the east. He was still convinced that he could find a sea passage to India and China. It was left to men like Cortes to explore the lands that Columbus had found.

Twelve years after Columbus landed on the island of Hispaniola, Hernan Cortes, a young man of nineteen, came out to settle on the island. Like other young men of the time, many of whom were younger sons of Spanish noblemen, he hoped to make his fortune. He had introductions to some of the government people in the main town on the island and, after a while, 9 they granted him an estate and a number of natives to work on his land. It was rapidly becoming the custom to employ the Indian natives on the lands of the Spanish settlers. At first they were persuaded to help in building houses and churches with friendly promises and gifts of beads but, before they knew what was happening to them, they had become slaves in their own land.

When Cortes was twenty-six, he joined an expedition to conquer the neighbouring island of Cuba and brought it under Spanish rule. He stayed in Cuba for eight years and became one of the wealthiest landowners. He did not take part in any of the expeditions which were gradually exploring the coastline of America, but he took a great deal of interest in them. When one of the expeditions came back with the news that they had heard of a rich country called Mexico, Cortes's imagination was fired. The men who had been there spoke of gold and jewellery which they had found in a great stone temple. They had been told of a floating city and a great emperor living beyond the mountains. Mexico sounded like a rich prize and Cortes knew that it must be his.

He was related by marriage to the governor of Cuba and he persuaded the governor to let him have command of an expedition to conquer Mexico. Cortes seemed a good choice – he was courageous, took his religion seriously and, besides, he was wealthy, which was extremely important if he was to make a success of it since the commander of an expedition had to pay many of the costs himself. It was expensive for the soldiers who joined as well. They had to pay their own passage on the ship and had to buy their own weapons and a horse if they could. They even had to pay a doctor's fee when they were ill or wounded. But the young men of Cuba seemed willing to risk anything for Cortes. They admired his bravery and trusted him as a leader.

Cortes collected men to join him partly by writing letters to people he knew and partly by means of a *proclamation*. He had a banner made and town criers went through the streets beating drums and blowing trumpets. They announced that anyone

Don ferdinando cordes jng; 1 5 z 9 seiner
alters   Jm 4 z diser hat der kay
agten   karowe dem funfften
herr   auch gann zj judian
             gewunnen.

Cortes

who would go with Cortes to the newly discovered land to conquer and settle would receive a share of the silver and gold, and would be given an estate and Indians to help work the land. On the banners were the words: 'Brothers and comrades, let us follow the sign of the Holy Cross in true faith, for under this sign we shall conquer.' For the Spaniards believed that they were going on a kind of crusade to bring Christianity to the people of the new country. God, they were convinced, was sending them.

All the young men who joined the expedition had farms and they brought all the provisions they could for the journey. Their wives made them clothes and cotton-padded armour, which was better than metal armour in the hot climate of the area. Cortes gave orders to the soldiers to sharpen their swords and to get blacksmiths to make helmets and arrows. In fact, to be on the safe side, Cortes asked two blacksmiths to come with him. Apart from soldiers, there were also priests who conducted mass and later baptised the Indians, a lawyer who advised Cortes whether certain actions were lawful, and a few servants, among whom were a number of negroes who had originally come from Spain with the first settlers. When the expedition was ready to leave, it consisted of 11 ships, carrying 508 swordsmen, 100 sailors (who did not fight), 32 crossbowmen, 13 musketeers and 16 horses; also 14 cannons, with powder and spare parts. The horses were particularly valuable, as one of the soldiers wrote: 'At that time negroes and horses were worth their weight in gold and the reason why we had no more horses was that there were none to be bought.' Cortes also laid in a stock of Spanish cloth and glass beads which could be used for presents to the Indians.

The expedition was now complete and set sail from Cuba on 10 February 1519. In a few days it landed on the tip of Mexico in an area called the Yucatan. This part of the country was inhabited by the *Mayas*, a tribe outside the Aztec *empire*. The nearest point on the coast is only 140 kilometres from Cuba and two ships had already touched on the coast before but had not explored further into Mexico. In fact, the year before Cortes's

The conquistadors building their ships

13

expedition, Spaniards had been to the Yucatan and had seen the Mayas. The stories they came back with – of gold and stone temples and a magnificent empire – had turned the eyes of the Spaniards towards Mexico and had resulted in Cortes's expedition.

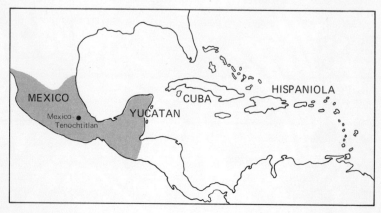

Position of Mexico

To Cortes and his men Mexico must have seemed like a New World indeed, with customs and a way of life that was quite different from Europe. They must have wondered where these strange people came from and how they had settled in their country.

2 Who Were the Mexicans?

We don't know for certain where the Mexicans came from. In the first place there were many different Mexican tribes; there were the Mayas, the Chichimecs, the Mixtecs, the Olmecs, the Zapotecs, the Huastecs, the Totonacs, the Tabascans and the Toltecs, as well as the Aztecs who were the most important tribe. We think they probably all came from the same place originally – from Asia.

The first men seem to have appeared in the Americas between ten and fifteen thousand years ago during the fourth Ice Age. The map below shows that Asia and America are divided

Man crosses from Asia to America

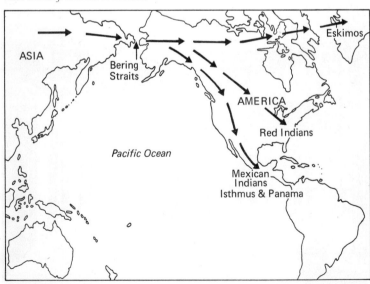

by the *Bering Straits*. The straits are 90 kilometres wide and there are three islands in between the two continents.

In the Ice Age the level of the sea was lower than it is now, so the islands would have been larger and nearer to each other than they are now. Perhaps they were only 40 kilometres apart. In winter men could have crossed from island to island over the ice. (In summer they could not cross as the ice would have cracked in places.) But why should they want to cross over these land bridges? Probably they crossed almost accidentally while following the animals which were their livelihood. As the fourth Ice Age was gradually coming to an end the animals

A Mayan Indian wearing the ancient costume of the Dance of the Flyers

which depended on cold climates move north and east and the *nomadic* bands of hunters followed them. They may have crossed the Bering Straits without being aware that they were crossing to a new continent. Many hundreds of tribes must have crossed to America in this way before the ice sheets melted and so cut America off from Asia. America became isolated and developed in quite a different way, without influences from the outside world.

Look at the two pictures below. The features of the Mexican Indians are very similar to Asiatic features. This seems to support the idea that the first Americans crossed from Asia.

An Indian tribesman at a dance festival near Delhi, India

For thousands of years the hunters wandered in various directions. Some went further north following the animals. These are the Eskimos. Some discovered the buffalo and followed it into the interior of North America. These are the Red Indians who now live on Indian Reservations in the U.S.A. Other tribes went further south; some as far as South America, some to the Isthmus of Panama, and some ended their wanderings to settle in the fertile valley of Mexico.

A hunting tribe cannot settle because its life depends on following its prey. In the valley of Mexico the hunters probably hunted large beasts such as *mammoths*, in much the same way as prehistoric men caught animals in the rest of the world. They used to force the beast into a trap by making wild noises to frighten it. Then they would capture it as shown in the picture.

Capturing a mammoth

But this was a hard existence because sometimes beasts might not be seen for days. Gradually men began to realise that they could be more sure of having food to eat if they cultivated the land so the Indians began to learn how to farm. This was about seven thousand years ago. At first they lived on wild plants and gradually they learnt how to sow crops and reap a harvest. In the valley of Mexico they discovered *maize* (corn on the cob) and this is still the basic food crop of Mexico today. The important point about maize is that it does not seed itself but must be *cultivated*. This meant that a tribe which depended on corn for its existence had to settle in one place for a long time. It was not easy to cultivate the land in Mexico as it was a very mountainous country, and there was a great deal of desert land. But, once it had settled, a tribe could learn how to grow food in more difficult places. It would get larger and a *civilisation* would begin to form.

One of the most interesting of these early groups of settlers were the Mayas. At one point in their wanderings they may have settled in the fertile Valley of Mexico, but their farming methods were very primitive and they used to exhaust the land by growing crops on it every year rather than allowing it to lie *fallow* and so regain its strength. When they had exhausted the land, they moved and this drove the tribe further and further south until they finally settled in the area which is now the Yucatan, Quintana Roo, British Honduras and Guatemala. Look back to the map on page 14. The Mayas settled in this area in about 2000 BC, and they kept to their own way of life for 3,700 years! Other kingdoms rose and fell in the fertile valley and, although some of them, especially the Toltecs, brought their customs as far as the Mayan country, they were never able to conquer it. Even the Spaniards found it a difficult task, and the Mayas were not subdued until many years after the rest of Mexico had come under Spanish rule.

If you go to the country of the Mayas today the sights you see there are almost as wonderful as the first vision the Spaniards had. There are many temples and ancient cities hidden in the depths of the jungle. Many are still overgrown with trees

Typical scenery of the dry highlands of Mexico

and have yet to be explored. Some cannot be reached by road; only on horseback or along a narrow river. In parts the jungle is so thick around the temples that you have to cut it away before you can pass.

The pyramid of the Inscriptions at Palenque

It seems amazing that the Mayas should have built their cities in such wild country. We do not know for certain why they did. Some say that they were driven away from the more fertile areas of Mexico and were forced into the jungle look-ing for water to feed their animals and water their crops. If you look at a relief map of Mexico you will see that there are very few rivers in the flat area of the Yucatan. Maya tribes set-tled by the rivers where they could, but many wandered further

The sacred Well at Chichen Itza where prisoners were sacrificed to the rain god

into the jungle where they found natural wells hollowed out of limestone. Some were as much as 60 metres across with the water 30 metres below the surface.

As water was so precious, the Mayas worshipped the rain and *sacrificed* prisoners to the rain god by throwing them into a sacred well. They could not swim, so hardly any of them survived, but one man did not drown. His name was Kukulcan, and the Mayas were so impressed that they took him out of the well next day. He proved a brave man and they chose him as their leader. He founded the city of *Chichen Itza*, and made peace among the tribes of the Yucatan. Then one day, as suddenly as he had come, he disappeared. Afterwards the Mayas worshipped him as a god.

Places like Chichen Itza were religious cities. Only the temples and ceremonial palaces were built out of stone. The people lived in mud huts scattered round the religious centre. In fact, the common people could not go into the temples as this was a privilege only allowed to the priests.

The largest pyramid at Chichen Itza. The Spaniards called it El Castillo which means 'the castle'

The temples were built on top of pyramids. Everyone knows about the Egyptian pyramids built around 3000 BC, but not so many people are familiar with the Maya (and Aztec) pyramids, built around AD 600 to 900. They are different from the Egyptian pyramids, which were built as tombs and had pointed tops. The Maya pyramids have a flat top on which a temple was built. The steps up the side are extremely steep and narrow. Some were at an angle of about 55 degrees to the ground. (Compare this with the angle of your stairs at home.)

The pyramid was made by piling up a mound of earth and rubble. It was then covered with cut stone and cemented with mortar made by burning limestone.

Another kind of building in the religious cities was the *observatory*. The priest in a primitive tribe was also an *astrologer*; the people relied on him to foretell changes in weather which would affect the crops. From the observatories the priests watched the movement of the stars and planets and they developed a very complicated calendar.

Actually they had three calendars. The first was called 'haab' and divided the year into 365 days. There were eighteen months each with twenty days. This gave 360 days, leaving five extra days which were thought to be unlucky. In these days before the old year died the people did no work but waited to see if the new year would renew itself. Children born in these five days were considered unlucky. The Egyptians had a similar calendar.

The second calendar, called 'tzolkin', showed the sacred year, and was used for reckoning the feasts of the gods. This was divided into 260 days. If you imagine two *cog-wheels*, you will see how these calendars worked together (see picture). One was divided into 360 parts and the other into 260. To find out on which day a religious festival fell on the 'haab' calendar, knowing its day on the religious calendar, you would turn the wheels until the festival day matched a day on the 'haab' wheel. Now the 260 day would turn more than once in each revolution of the large wheel, and so the festival would fall on a different day each year. But you would find that once in every fifty-two revolutions of the big wheel – that is every fifty-two normal

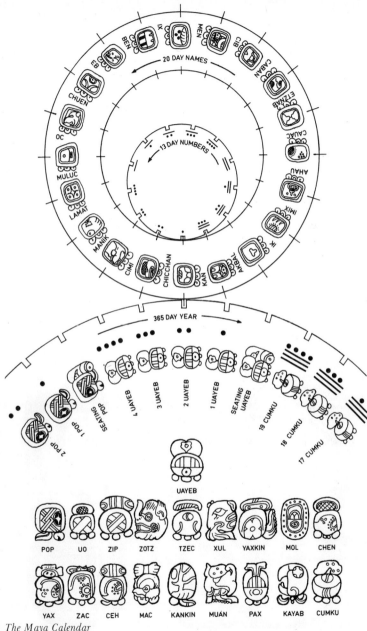

The Maya Calendar

years – that the festival would fall on the same day as before. The fifty-two-year period was called the Calendar Round.

The third calendar was called the 'long count', and was used for referring to a day in the past. Every single day from the beginning of time was counted and, to refer to a date in the past, you simply counted backwards to find its number. The beginning of time, as far as the Mayas were concerned, was 3111 BC by our calendar. We do not know what happened on this day to make it an important day in Maya history.

Look at the picture of the calendar wheels again. The small drawings round the outer edge show the Maya picture writing. These are called *hieroglyphs*, and, here again, is an interesting parallel with the ancient Egyptians who also used hieroglyphic writing. The Maya writing was quite different, as you can see if you compare this picture of a Maya hieroglyph with the ancient Egyptian writings.

A Maya hieroglyph

Egyptian hieroglyphs

The face in the Maya hieroglyph is very unusual as they had some strange ideas about beauty. They thought flat heads gave people a 'noble air' and, as soon as a baby was born, they flattened his head by tying it within two boards. Of course, this was very useful later as a flat head made it easier to carry heavy loads! Many Mayas were cross-eyed as they thought this was a special mark of beauty. Mothers hung a ball in front of their children's eyes so that both eyes *focused* on the ball and so began to cross. Apart from these artificial features, the Mayas, who are still living in the Yucatan today, look much as they did when the wall painting in the picture was done. They do not, of course, wear such complicated clothes or such strange headdresses, but the traditional costume is a straight smock which is still worn.

A wall painting in a Mayan temple. The scene shows warriors celebrating a victory

It looks as if the Mayas had reached about the same point of civilisation in AD 900 as the Egyptians had in 3000 BC. The gap of time between the two civilisations is amazingly long, but we must remember that the first men of the Americas were hunters and then became nomadic farmers. They settled much later than the Egyptians in a land that was not so fertile. They also had no contact with the outside world at all, whereas Egypt received ideas from other groups of people settling around the Mediterranean.

3 The Aztecs and their Empire

When the conquistadors came to Mexico, the Aztecs were the ruling tribe, and that is why most people remember the Aztecs when they think of ancient Mexico.

Like the other tribes, the ancestors of the Aztecs came across the Bering Straits, and probably lived somewhere in the north for a time. But they were a nomadic tribe and wandered from place to place in search of fertile lands. According to an old

Picture writing from an Aztec manuscript recording how the City of Mexico-Tenochtitlan was founded

legend, one of their gods encouraged them to go south and said that they would one day found a large city on a swamp. The god told them that they would find an eagle sitting on a cactus, eating a serpent, and that this would be the place where they would build their city. The eagle and serpent are now the symbol of the present Republic of Mexico.

The Aztecs wandered for many hundreds of years looking for a place to settle. Some historians say that they began their wanderings from a place called Aztlan and that this is why they are called the Aztecs. As you can imagine, it was not an easy life being a member of a tribe that was always moving from place to place, even if it was a strong and brave tribe as the Aztecs were. Actually, the fact that they were fierce in war made things more difficult for them as the larger and more powerful tribes drove them away out of jealousy and because the Aztecs were taking their food. One neighbouring chieftain tried to make friends with the Aztecs by giving his daughter in marriage to their chief. The Aztecs had a very strange way of showing their gratitude.

The symbol of the Republic of Mexico today

They felt that, if they were to kill the girl as a sacrifice, this would show the chieftain that they realised it was a great honour, but that they felt they were unworthy of it, so they killed the girl, and invited the chieftain to what was to have been the wedding feast. You can imagine his feelings! The Aztecs had to escape to an island in the middle of a lake to avoid his revenge. This was a large lake in the Valley of Mexico and there, in a cave, they saw the eagle, serpent and cactus of the legend, and knew that this was the place where they must build their capital. This was in the year 1325. They were, by that time, accustomed to hardship and work and, although the place was a swampy island, miles from the mainland, they were not afraid to begin the task of building a city. It was quite an undertaking!

When the Aztecs arrived on the island, they had no means of buying stone or timber to build their city, so they began by trading the fish and water animals they caught for what they needed to build their town. They made the island larger by building great rafts of reeds and covering these with layers of mud which baked hard in the sun. The lake was quite shallow and they were able to anchor the platforms to the bottom by planting trees on the platforms whose roots grew into the bed of the lake. The first houses were made of sticks covered with mud and a thin layer of lime plaster on top. There were no windows and the whole family lived in one dark room. Sometimes a coarse cloth curtain divided the room. Many huts in Mexico today are still made like this. They are called 'adobe' huts.

Over the cave where they had seen the eagle and serpent of the legend, they built a temple to the god who had told them that they should settle on this spot. In time, they built temples to their other gods in a huge ceremonial square, which is still the centre of Mexico City today.

In England this was the time of the great cathedral builders and Salisbury was finished around 1330. (You can read about Salisbury in Then and There: 'The Medieval Town'.) The cathedral builders could build more complicated buildings than the Aztecs because they had better materials. They had metal tools with which to cut the stone and to carve designs in it, whereas

A Mexican Indian home today. These mud huts have remained unchanged for hundreds of years

the Aztecs had no metal tools and had to use sharp flints. The English builders had carts to carry stone from one place to another and pulleys to *hoist* it up so they could build high towers, but the Aztecs had not discovered the wheel, let alone the pulley, and so did not know that it could be used as a piece of simple machinery. So they had to carry stone across the lake in canoes, and drag it along the ground with ropes – rather like the builders of Stonehenge.

All the same, they built a very beautiful city. There were temples built on the tops of high pyramids, for the worship of all the important gods. There were palaces for the Aztec leaders and chief citizens of the tribe as well as houses for the common people, and market places in the city squares. One of the

The main square of Mexico-Tenochtitlan looked like this

conquistadors seeing the city for the first time was amazed at its beauty and described it as follows:

> These great temples and buildings rising from the water, all made of stone, seemed like an enchanted vision from the tale of Amadis. Indeed, some of our soldiers asked whether it was not all a dream. It was all so wonderful that I do not know how to describe the first glimpse of things never heard of, seen or dreamed of before.

The name of the city was *Mexico-Tenochtitlan*. It was called Mexico because, in Aztec language, this meant 'the town in the middle of the moon (or lake)'. It also had the name Tenochtitlan because this was very like the name for the hard-fruited prickly pear that grows in this region. The city was something 33 like Venice today. There were canals between the houses and people could only get to and fro by canoe. Some houses could only be approached by a drawbridge which was lowered to allow people to enter. These houses were usually only one storey high, and had flat roofs which were used as fighting places for warriors defending the city. About 90,000 people lived in the city, which is quite a large number compared to London at the same time, which had only 40,000 inhabitants.

The island city was connected to the mainland by three *causeways*, which were roads built across the lake. These were very straight, like Roman roads, and they were wide enough for eight people to march side by side. At various points there were drawbridges connecting sections of the causeways, which could be raised or taken away so that the Aztecs could prevent their enemies from entering the city.

The defences of the Aztec capital were better than most walled medieval cities in Europe. An enemy army had to cross one of the three causeways, the shortest of which was 3 kilometres long. This gave the Aztecs plenty of time to pull up the drawbridges and so block the way. They could also attack the warriors on the causeway with arrows shot from their canoes. An

A view of the city in the middle of the lake

army walking eight *abreast* presented an easy target. The result was that tribes nearby were afraid to attack the Aztecs, whereas the Aztecs went on frequent expeditions to bring neighbouring tribes under their rule. It had taken them fifty years to become a power feared by other states. At first the Aztecs formed an alliance with their more powerful neighbours, the cities of *Tlacopan* and *Texcoco* and, whatever wealth was gained from tribes they conquered was shared out between these three cities, but, as Mexico-Tenochtitlan grew more powerful, it was finally able to seize most of the wealth and to rule at the head of a large empire.

Most states build up an empire either by picking a quarrel with their weaker neighbours and conquering them by force, or by going on an expedition to bring their own civilisation to another tribe or country. In these ways the Aztecs conquered thirty-eight provinces before, in their turn, their empire was conquered by the Spaniards. The Aztec army was much stronger than the armies of other tribes and was also better organised, probably because the years of wandering had made them very tough and courageous. They always fought their battles in the same way. They didn't try to kill their enemies in battle, but took them prisoners if they could, and these prisoners became victims for sacrifice to the gods. They then forced the chieftains of the conquered tribe to accept the Aztec emperor as overlord and to send frequent *tribute* to the capital as a sign of goodwill. These tributes were very high indeed, and left the state which paid them extremely poor, so the Aztecs were not liked. Every so often a tax-collector went to collect the tribute. If the tribe was unwilling to pay, the tax-collector reported back to the emperor, and an army was sent down to subdue the tribe again.

It took two hundred years for the empire of the Aztecs to reach the size that it was under *Montezuma*, who was emperor when Cortes landed. It was not a very secure empire because the Aztecs ruled through terror, holding their weaker neighbours down by making them fear war and pay heavy taxes. Even tribes which were not part of the empire hated the Aztecs. The *Tlaxcalans* were one of the strongest tribes and they had

A tribute sheet showing what goods were sent to the capital. This is another example of Aztec picture writing. The words were added later

resisted the Aztecs for years but, as they lived so near to Mexico-Tenochtitlan, they were frequently attacked. They had no way of hitting back because Mexico-Tenochtitlan was too well fortified.

By 1520 most of the tribes, many of whom had only recently come under Aztec rule, were ready to rebel. The Aztecs at Mexico-Tenochtitlan, on the other hand had been growing very rich as a result of the wars. All kinds of produce flowed into the capital – some of it obtained through taxes, and some through trade. Cotton, cocoa, skins, many-coloured feathers and silver came into the city. The important citizens could live in great luxury. Their clothes were richly decorated and they wore many gold ornaments round their necks, through their ears and sometimes through their noses. Their houses were furnished with beautiful mats and wooden furniture. One of the conquistadors noted with surprise that the goods sold in the market compared well with those in the richest markets in the world, such as Constantinople and Baghdad.

When gold mines were discovered in the province of *Zacatula*,

Extent of the Aztec empire under Montezuma

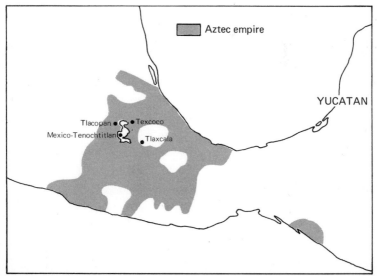

which was twelve days' journey from Mexico-Tenochtitlan, gold began to flow into the capital. Most of this was taken by the emperor as his personal share of the tribute. *Jade* was also very precious and was valued by some more highly than gold itself. The rest of the tribute goods – cotton, food, leather and woven goods – were shared out amongst the people according to their position in society.

Every citizen had to serve at some time as a warrior, because more warriors were needed to keep the subdued states in check as the empire grew. This meant that many farmers had to leave their homes and live for long periods in the lands of the tribes who were being kept down. All journeys were on foot, as they had no horses and no carts, and so were very tiring. Probably the Aztec warriors hated these expeditions as much as the tribes they bullied, but they had been brought up in the belief that their gods demanded war.

4 Religion

The gods demanded war; or rather, the Aztecs thought they did. They were afraid of their gods and believed that they would punish the people if they were not properly worshipped. This meant that the people of Mexico had to show their gods that they were willing to offer up human lives as the greatest sacrifice they could make to their gods. Wars were a necessary part of life because they gave all tribes an opportunity to take prisoners of war who could be offered to their gods. This is why they tried not to kill their enemy in battle, but to take him alive.

We know of other people who also practised human sacrifice. The Druids in England sometimes offered voluntary victims to their god. In ancient Greece a victim was sometimes killed to expel evil from the city, and in Africa and Oceania many forms of human sacrifice were known. But nowhere was it practised as much as in Mexico.

The Mexicans believed that human hearts were the 'food' of the gods and that unless they were offered enough they would grow angry and the world would come to an end. The Aztecs were particularly afraid of the sun god because he could stop the sun shining and so throw the land into darkness. They believed the only thing that made the sun rise in the morning was the daily offering to the god. We have always assumed that, because the sun has risen one morning, it will rise again the next, but, for the Aztecs, there was no such certainty and they did not dare risk the god's anger.

Sacrifices were made at the top of high pyramids and there was an elaborate ceremony performed by the high priests. On special occasions there was music and dancing. Only the priests

The temple of the sun at Teotihuacan

were allowed on the steps of the pyramid, and they stood on platforms all the way up, while the people watched from below. On very important occasions the ceremony was carried out by the emperor himself.

When the Spaniards came to Mexico, they were horrified by the sacrifices they saw, but we must remember that the Christian religion itself was responsible for a great deal of cruelty in Europe at this time. The Spanish Inquisition burned disbelievers at the stake as an example to others, and the Aztecs would probably have been just as horrified by this, especially as victims might be condemned without a fair trial. There were only three ways in which a Mexican could become a victim for sacrifice. He could be a prisoner of war, a criminal who had been reduced to the level of a sacrificial slave, or he might be a voluntary victim who chose death. Curious as it may seem, there were many voluntary sacrifices. They were usually warriors who chose to die in glory or, sometimes, it might have been a great honour to have been chosen as the most handsome person in the village who was offered to the gods. Aztec beliefs were strong and made them behave like this. They thought that they had to choose between killing human beings and bringing about the end of the world. Probably they did not value human life as much as we do today.

There were hundreds of gods – each village had its own idols – but there were three main gods who ruled over the Mexicans. They were *Huitzilopochtli*, *Tezcatlipoca*, and *Quetzalcoatl*. As god of the sun, Huitzilopochtli, whose name means 'Humming-Bird Wizard', made the corn grow, and this was the chief crop of the Aztecs. At certain times of the year an image of

Huitzilopochtli,
god of the sun

the god was made in cornflour and was baked, decorated and eaten. Huitzilopochtili's most important function was as war god and he was consulted by priests skilled in the art of interpreting signs before wars were waged. This was the god that the Emperor Montezuma consulted when he heard of the arrival of the Spaniards.

Almost as important as Huitzilopochtli was Tezcatlipoca, who was god of the night and god of evil. His name means 'Smoking Mirror' and his high priests used to wear mirrors as part of their costume. When they wished to consult the god, they would smoke the mirror and read the pictures they saw in it. They thought these pictures were signs from the great god.

Tezcatlipoca, god of night and evil

Tezcatlipoca had one great festival which lasted forty days. There was much feasting and banqueting and this was one of the festivals on which a young man offered himself for sacrifice at the end of the celebration. For forty days he was dressed and worshipped as if he were the god himself. He was given rich clothes and beautiful wives. Music was played to him during great banquets at which he sat at the head of the table. If, at the end of forty days, he was sad at the thought of his coming death, the priests gave him a drug to make him happy again. So he died in glory, believing that he would go straight to the paradise in the east.

Quetzalcoatl, god of wind and life

There was one god who was, by tradition, against human sacrifice. His name was Quetzalcoatl, which means the 'Feathered Serpent', and he is very important for our story. Quetzalcoatl was the god of wind and he blew life into things. He was also the god of learning. There is an ancient legend that Quetzalcoatl had once appeared in human form as the king of the Toltec Mexicans, and that he had preached against human sacrifice. As he was the god of the wind of life, he wanted to preserve life. When he saw that the Mexicans took no notice of his teachings, he sailed away east in the direction of the sunrise, and said that he would reappear again on an anniversary of the year and would *re-establish* his rule.

There is a story about Quetzalcoatl that he once shot arrows into a tree and they stuck there in the form of a cross so, when the Spaniards arrived, bringing Christianity with them, the crucifix seemed familiar to many Indians as the sign of Quetzalcoatl.

There were also a number of important minor gods, such as *Tlaloc*, the god of rain, Xochipilli the god of flowers and pleasure, Xochiquetzal goddess of the earth, and many other gods with equally unpronounceable names. Tlaloc was quite important because he controlled the floods, droughts, hail and lightning. The Aztecs thought he lived on the tops of high mountains where the rain clouds formed. He was feared because, in Mexico, it rains either too much or too little. This meant that, in Mexico-Tenochtitlan, there was constant fear of drought in the dry season and of flooding in the rainy season. There was one great flood which had destroyed a great part of the city and the Aztecs thought they could stop this happening again if they paid proper attention to Tlaloc. Very recently a statue of Tlaloc was moved from a village very near Mexico-City to the museum in the capital. The villagers say that, for fourteen days after this, it rained without stopping.

The temples of all these gods were richly decorated with stone carvings and paintings. The carvings round the foot of the temple were painted in many colours. It must have been a splendid sight to watch the priests dressed in long black cloaks disappearing over the top of the pyramid into the temple.

44

Today, when you stand at the foot of these pyramids, you cannot see the top. They were purposely built like this so that it looked to the people as if the priests were climbing straight up into the heavens where the gods were. Round the top and bottom of the pyramids were carvings of fierce snakes' heads, or *jackals*, or tigers. It is not surprising that the Aztecs were afraid of the gods.

One of the most amazing things about the stone carvings and statues was that they were done without metal tools. In ancient America there had been no bronze age or metal age as there

A stone statue from a temple at Chichen Itza

was in Europe, and people did not know how to make metal tools. So they used flints and tools made of very hard stone. They were extremely sharp and the craftsmen were able to make sculptures as good as any done with metal tools. In fact, one of the conquistadors said that there were painters and carvers in the city who were so remarkable that, if they had been living in the same society as *Michelangelo*, they would have been counted in the same rank. Michelangelo was alive at the time of the conquest and had already done some of his most famous sculptures (he was born in 1475).

Aztec sculpture of the eagle knight

Some of the most beautiful things made by the Aztecs were for their gods. Every home had an altar and craftsmen made small clay idols which were worshipped by the family. They kept their houses neat and tidy to honour the god, keeping the area round the altar especially clean. Even the squares where the great temples were were swept daily.

Craftsmen were also employed to make the rich feathered head-dresses that the high priests wore on special occasions. One of these was given to Cortes when he landed. It was the head-dress of the god Quetzalcoatl. The art of making these

Michelangelo's sculpture of a saint

47

The feathered headdress given to Cortes by Montezuma

head-dresses was to tie the stems of coloured feathers into the robe worn with it as it was being woven. They made patterns of birds or animals or, sometimes, just patterns. Later they used to make landscape pictures by this method. They were called 'feather *mosaics*'.

The temples were often decorated inside with fine wall paintings. There are hardly any of the Aztec paintings left now, but we can see from what remains that they used vivid colours. They usually showed battles at which the god of war had helped the tribe to overcome its enemies.

Music and dancing were also part of religious festivals. One of the most exciting dances, performed not far from the capital, was the Dance of the Flyers. Men dressed themselves up as

86.

Feather work. The feathers are tied together and woven into a pattern

The Dance of the Flyers. If you look back to page 16 you can see a man wearing the traditional costume of this dance

birds and 'flew' round a pole. This is still done in some parts of Mexico today.

So religion in Mexico was responsible for encouraging the arts and crafts, just as in Europe music, architecture and painting were encouraged by the Church. The Aztecs thought they should pay respect to their gods by making fine buildings and well-carved idols. When Cortes tried to tell Montezuma that Christianity was a finer religion, Montezuma replied:

> Throughout all time we have worshipped our own gods and thought they were good. I do not doubt the goodness of the god whom you worship but, if he is good for Spain, our gods are equally good for Mexico, so do not trouble to speak of them at present.

5 Aztec Society

The lives of Aztec people centred on religion, for the purpose of religion was to please the gods who kept all the planets moving and to arrange how to live on this planet. The priests who were skilled in reading signs could tell at your birth whether you would succeed or fail; whether you would win glory in war or whether you were born under an evil star and so could not avoid falling into wicked ways. People were so influenced by these *predictions* that they led their lives according to the expectations they had. Everyone believed he had a place in the world and he looked to the priests to tell him what it was.

Look at the diagram showing the different classes in Aztec society. As you can see, it is pyramid-shaped, like their temples.

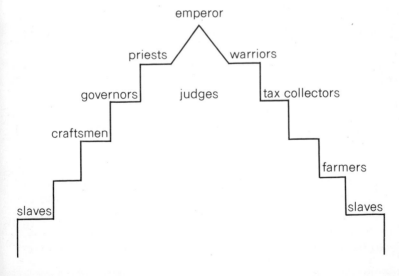

The emperor is at the head of the social order and the slaves at the bottom. Usually people inherited their social position from their fathers, but this was not always the case. For instance, the daughter of one of the emperors fell in love with a farmer and married him. Because of this royal marriage, he became lord of his village.

The priests, as you can see in the diagram, were on the second step of the pyramid and were very powerful. If you had been a young Aztec you would probably have been terrified of the priests. In the first place, you weren't allowed near them because, in the ceremony, they stood on the temple steps while you would have had to watch from the square below. Then, they looked odd with their black robes and hair that was matted with blood from the sacrifices. Sometimes they had a wild look in their eyes when they had been fasting in preparation for some important festival. But you would have respected the priests almost as much as the gods themselves. To you, a priest would have seemed to be the god himself because he could do magic.

There were ordinary priests and high priests. The ordinary priests were called *quacuilli* and they were the ones who sang or danced or beat the drum at religious festivals. They also served at their local temples. The more important priests were called *tlenamacac* and they performed the ceremonies in the great temple square at Mexico-Tenochtitlan. They were very important people and at their head were two priests who were as powerful as each other. One was the priest of Quetzalcoatl and the other was the priest of Huitzilopochtli. These men were advisers to the emperor.

Women could be priestesses and were sometimes *dedicated* to the temples at birth. They were in charge of the ceremonies to the goddesses.

Also on the second step of the pyramid diagram are the warriors. They were as important as the priests. In fact, most of the priests had been warriors when they were young. Every citizen in Mexico-Tenochtitlan either was a warrior or wanted to be one. The reason for this was that you could not gain respect until you had taken prisoners in battle. There were various ranks among the warriors which depended on the number of prisoners a man had taken. If he did not do well in battle he had to give up soldiering and devote himself to his piece of land. This meant he would never be able to wear dyed or embroidered clothes or any jewellery.

Aztec military costume

Fine clothes were for good fighters. When a man had taken four prisoners, he was allowed a share in the spoil that resulted from a campaign. After that he could become a chieftain and take part in councils of war. This meant he could wear a leather bracelet and feathered head-dress. The highest honour of all was to become one of the jaguar knights who were supposed to be the soldiers of the great god Tezcatlipoca. They wore the skin of a jaguar in battle. There was also an order of eagle knights. Look back to page 46 where there is a picture of an eagle knight. Can you see what he is wearing on his head?

The army of the Aztecs was commanded by four great military chiefs who were near relations of the emperor. Very often the new emperor was chosen from among these commanders. They were very rich and had gained their wealth through victories in battle. They were honoured, not for their possessions, but for the deeds that had made them rich. When the Spaniards came to Mexico, they thought these military chiefs formed a sort of nobility, and in a way they did, but they were not at all like the nobles who attended the courts of England, France or Spain. They did not pass on their wealth or titles to their sons, although sons of military commanders were able to receive a better education than sons of common men and so they rose to be commanders themselves.

Military leaders and those who gained high rank in battle were not only privileged by their clothes. They were also allowed to dance in pairs and each pair of warriors was joined by a girl with long flowing black hair. The dance went on for hours. Sometimes the emperor came and joined in. Look at the picture of an Aztec dance today. If you look carefully you can see a church in the background. Old habits are so deeply ingrained that, today, Mexicans revive their ancient dances on feast days of the Catholic Church.

On the third step of the pyramid diagram is the class of appointed officials. There were governors who looked after the affairs of cities all over the empire and within the capital. Mexico-Tenochtitlan was divided into four districts and each district had a governor who was called a *tecuhtli*. The tecuhtli

Traditions in Mexico are still kept up. Some dancers perform the ancient Aztec dances today

were elected but they usually came from the same family as the leader who had just died, so long as there was a suitable person – maybe a brother, or a nephew or a son; so it was a kind of *hereditary* honour, although it passed out of the family if the district did not feel that there was a responsible member of the family fit to rule. The governor saw that everyone in his district had a piece of land, and that young men were sent for military service. He saw that everyone received a fair share of the goods from subdued tribes that were shared out among the people. He made sure that taxes were collected and that the people under his care had a proper hearing before the judges.

This placed the governors in a slightly higher position than the other two kinds of official – the judges and the tax-collectors. The judges were chosen by the emperor and were sometimes selected from among the older officials and sometimes from the common people. A great deal of care was taken over choosing judges as it was a difficult job. A judge could lose his life if he allowed himself to be bribed or if he gave a wrong judgement. But there were always predictions to help a judge make up his mind and, if a man had expected from birth to fall into evil ways, no one would be very surprised to find him in court. One of the Spanish conquistadors was so impressed by the courts that he said he believed prisons were unnecessary. All you had to do was to draw a line and tell the prisoner to stay behind it, and he would. This was probably not quite true but it shows that the Aztecs were used to being kept in their places.

The tax-collectors were called the *calpixque*. They collected taxes from tributary tribes and sent reports to the emperor about the state of agriculture and trade in their area. If a famine broke out, it was up to the tax-collector to tell the emperor and make sure that his area did not have to pay taxes until it could afford to.

These were the ruling men of Aztec society. Who did they rule over?

There were the craftsmen; we read about them in the last chapter. Many of the goldsmiths, feather-workers and builders worked at the emperor's court and they were in a position of privileged servants; very similar, in fact, to artists at the courts of Europe at this time. They were well paid and honoured according to their skills. On one occasion, fourteen sculptors were commissioned to make a statue of the great Montezuma, and each was paid with clothes for himself and his wife, ten loads of beans, two loads each of peppers, cocoa and cotton and a boatful of maize. This was before the work was started. When it was finished, each man got two slaves, two more loads of cocoa, and a load of salt.

The craftsmen were one step higher than the common people in the social pyramid because they at least had a few privileges whereas the common people had none. Although there were a great many priests, warriors and officials of all kinds, most of the people were farmers. The farming class was called the *maceualli*. It was they who worked on the common lands and provided maize for the city. They also had their own plot of land which was given to them when they got married and set up a home, and this plot went back to the state when the farmer died. The plots were inside the city, as cities then were not completely built up areas as they are now.

The farmer had a vote in the elections for the governor of the district, but he also had to give services to the district. He had to help with communal work such as building the great temples and roads, keeping the district clean and fetching drinking water for the palace officials. There was also military service which gave the farmer the opportunity to fight so bravely that he could rise out of his class and become a warrior.

The farmer was hardworking, but he was a free man and could own slaves, who were the lowest class of all. The slaves were called *tlacotli*. There were many ways of becoming a slave. Prisoners of war who were not sacrificed in the temples were sold as slaves but, strangely enough, most of them were voluntary slaves who had sold themselves to another person. They actually preferred to have someone else look after them in return for such services as working in the fields or in the house, cooking the meals and sewing cloth into garments for their owners. A person who sold himself received his price in the   57

Slaves working in the fields

presence of four respected citizens. This was twenty pieces of cloth and he was free until he had spent it all. This usually took about a year. Then he gave himself up to his master. Families would sell their children in this way.

The owner treated his slaves like his own children. They did not suffer the brutal treatment that was given to slaves after the conquest, nor did they live in the miserable way that some of the African slaves in the southern states of America did later. If a slave wanted to free himself, it was not too difficult. If he could break away from his master and run to the palace he would be free because, once inside the palace gates, the royal presence of the emperor would free him. In fact, if anyone prevented a runaway slave from getting into the palace, he might be forced into slavery himself. Another way was to buy oneself out of slavery. The slave could earn a little money by doing extra work and could pay back his master the price originally paid. This made it possible for a man who had been sold into slavery when young to break away and make a better life for himself. He might gain military honours. There was even one emperor who was the son of a slave girl.

Who, then, was the emperor who was the head of this great pyramid of Aztec society? You will remember, when we were talking about the governors of districts, that they were elected leaders, but that they usually came from the same family. It was the same with the emperor. On the death of an emperor, the high priests and military commanders got together and chose a successor. It had to be the person in the royal family who was bravest in war and most knowledgeable in matters of religion. Usually they chose a brother or a nephew and sometimes the son of the old emperor.

The man who was elected emperor in 1503 was Montezuma II, nephew of the last ruler, and it was he who was emperor when Cortes landed. He was exceptionally brave – his name means 'Courageous Lord' – and was very skilled in interpreting the signs of the gods. One of the soldiers in Cortes's expedition, called Bernal Diaz, described Montezuma:

> The great Montezuma was about forty years old, of good height, well proportioned, spare and slight, and not very dark though of the usual Indian complexion. His face was rather long and cheerful. He had fine eyes and, in his appearance and manner, could express *geniality* or, when necessary, a serious *composure*. The clothes he wore one day, he did not wear again till three or four days later. He had a guard of two hundred chieftains lodged in rooms besides his own; only some of whom were permitted to speak to him. When they entered his presence they were

compelled to take off their rich cloaks and put on ones of little value. They had to be clean and walk barefoot, with their eyes downcast, for they were not allowed to look him in the face and, as they approached, they had to make three *obeisances*, saying, as they did so, 'Lord, my lord, my great lord!'

Montezuma

Montezuma had a huge palace and a vast household. When his servants cooked for the emperor, they had to prepare more than three hundred plates of food for palace officials and chiefs, and more than a thousand for the guard. For each meal the servants prepared more than thirty dishes such as turkeys, pheasants, wild duck, venison, pigeons, hares and many other kinds of food that are familiar to us. The emperor sat at a low table which had a beautifully decorated screen placed in front so that no one should see the great Montezuma eat. Four of his advisers stood by his table and talked to him, but they were not allowed to look at him either. Occasionally, he would offer them a taste of whichever dish was best, but they had to eat it standing up. Four beautiful girls waited on Montezuma, and sometimes a hunchbacked dwarf would be at the meal to amuse him, like a court jester. After the meal the emperor would drink a cup of chocolate, a drink which fascinated the Spaniards who had not known chocolate in any form. We owe our fondness for chocolate today to the discovery of Mexico.

The expenses of the emperor, who had to feed so many people every day as well as giving rich gifts to his advisers and paying his workmen, were very great. This is why the emperor took for himself gold and precious things collected from the tribes as tribute tax, before he let the rest be shared out among the officials and the people. Under Montezuma, the empire grew bigger, and there were 371 tribes paying tribute tax to the capital. Montezuma was, therefore, very rich and very powerful.

But Montezuma faced a problem that no other Aztec emperor had ever been troubled with. White men had been seen in the Maya country, and reports of the two expeditions which came before Cortes had reached the emperor. Montezuma knew that something dreadful was going to happen. It was not simply that white men had been seen. He was a powerful man and was equal to fighting with any tribe, but there were a number of evil *omens* during his reign. A baby with two heads was born; the volcano *Popocatepetl*, which had been quiet for years, suddenly erupted; a sign had been seen in the heavens;

priests were having dreams foretelling a dreadful future. Montezuma was as skilled as any high priest at interpreting these signs. To him it meant that disaster was near and that there was little or nothing he could do to avoid it. The ancient legends about the return of the god Quetzalcoatl were remembered, and the anniversary of the year on which he was to come back was approaching. So, while Cortes was getting together his expedition in Cuba, Montezuma was surrounding himself with astrologers and magicians to find out what he had to do to win back the favour of the gods.

An omen in the sky. The Aztecs thought this meant that disaster was near

What Montezuma thought was of great importance, because he was at the head of the social pyramid, and so his word was law. He had only to order men for a military campaign, and his officials would see that soldiers were supplied but, if he chose not to make use of his army, the people below him had to trust that he knew what he was doing. They did trust him because they believed he received his power from the gods and so would not lead them badly.

6 Daily Life

Imagine you are a young Aztec living at the time of the great Montezuma. Let's say you belong to the family of one of the officials of Mexico-Tenochtitlan because then you would have a better education than the common people.

Your family house is made of stone, and there is one main room. Maybe, if your family is very wealthy, you might have more rooms and, however well off you were, you would have a small *shrine* where you could worship the family gods. Your uncle's or cousin's houses would be next door to yours, and all the houses of one family would be grouped round the same courtyard.

Inside the house, everyone sleeps in the same room on a coarse mat which becomes a chair in the daytime. There is very little furniture – perhaps a carved wooden chest and some embroidered hangings. You get up early because it is very hot in Mexico so no one likes to waste the cool hours of the early morning. There will be a canal by the front of your house, and you will bathe every morning in the lake, using the fruit of a tree that the Spaniards called the 'soap tree' to wash yourself with. It isn't really soap but it produces a lather which is good enough for washing. Clothes are washed with this fruit too. If you are a boy you will be wearing a short cloak tied at the shoulder. When you reach the age of thirteen you will wear a loincloth which is tied round the waist and in between the legs with tassled ends dangling at front and back. If you are a girl you wear a white embroidered smock and a long or short skirt with embroidery on the hem. Your long black hair is tied in loops on the top of your head so that it looks a bit like horns.

There will be no breakfast but, maybe after a few hours of work, at about ten o'clock, you might get a bowl of maize porridge, sweetened with honey. Maize is the chief food of all Mexico so at most of the meals maize is served in one form or another. If you are a girl, you will then stay in the house and help your mother to prepare *tortillas*, which are thin pancakes of maize flour. Mexicans still eat tortillas rather than bread. It is quite a long process to make them and takes up a large part of the day. First, the corn has to be stripped from the cob, then it is left to soak for a while in water to get soft. After that it is pounded into a thick paste with a pestle and mortar. When the dough is ready, a small ball is rolled in the palm of the hand and is then clapped from one hand to the other until a thin round pancake is formed. Some girls are so good at clapping tortillas that they can get them to a size of 25 centimeters across. The tortillas are then cooked on a flat earthenware disc over a charcoal fire. Maize tortillas are eaten for lunch which is the main meal and is in the middle of the day. Beans, green peppers and pieces of meat are rolled up inside the tortilla, eaten with a hot tomato sauce.

A mother and daughter clapping tortillas and cooking them

You would also go with your mother to the local market to buy food and, if she needs anything for the house, you might go to the great market square of *Tlatelolco*. There, you could trade for shoes, ropes, jaguar skins, eagle feathers, cloth, straw mats, gold and silver. There are several streets in the market, each one dealing with one kind of merchandise. There is a street selling meat, another selling beans, another selling birds, and so on. About 25,000 people come to the market every day. They do not use money to buy things but trade with cocoa beans, feathers or a cylinder of powdered gold. For example, you would pay a hundred cocoa beans to have a canoe full of drinking water brought to your home. Do you see now why Montezuma partly paid his sculptors with cocoa beans? (See page 57.)

The market is very well organised and there is a building in the middle of the square where judges sit all day and solve market disputes. There are also men who watch what goes on. They make sure proper weights and measures are used and that no one is treated unfairly. They form a kind of market police. The market is run by the merchants, who were not mentioned in the last chapter because they do not fit into the structure of Aztec society. Because of their wandering life, merchants are a class on their own. They have their own gods, priests and judges. They are still ruled by the emperor but they are in a slightly privileged position.

Some of the market goods come from the merchants who trade with tribes outside the empire, and some of the goods are a part of the taxes collected from the empire. Most of the tax is shared among the people so only the luxury goods appear in the markets.

The rest of your day is devoted to weaving and embroidery. You might even be making your wedding dress, though you wouldn't know who you were going to marry. As a girl, you might get a small amount of education if your parents take you to a temple. There, you would learn about religion as well as domestic arts, and you would learn to keep your place. You are not supposed to talk unless you are asked a question, and then your answer should be as short as possible. If you were to make

Model of a scene in an Aztec market

a remark such as 'A drum is playing, I wonder where they are singing and dancing?', you would be punished severely. You would be forbidden to talk to boys at all and the whole family would be disgraced if you exchanged a few words with a boy you met in the street.

If you are a boy, life is a little freer, though there is a lot of hard studying. Let us say the priests had read the signs on your birth and had told your parents that you were born under a lucky star and would become one of the emperor's advisers. Your father would almost certainly send you to the nearest religious school, called a *calmecac*, which gives a training for the priesthood. He would do this, not because he thought you would become a priest, but because the calmecac offers the best education. There, you would learn religion, morals, history, singing and dancing; how to fix the times of the religious festivals, how to read the picture writing, the use of herbs, and many other things.

One of the most important things you would learn is how the calendar works. We have already seen how the Maya Calendar worked (see page 25). The Aztec system was very similar. They also had a year of 365 days divided into eighteen months of twenty days, with five unlucky days tagged on at the end. Each day of the month had a name, just as we name days of the week, and the whole year was named after the first day in the year. One of these names was Reed. In a Reed year, the name of the first day in every month was Reed but, at the end of the year, you went on naming the days after Reed during the five unlucky days. This meant that the first day of the next year was given the name of the day five days after Reed, which was Flint. In the year after Flint, the year began on the day House and, in the fourth year, it began on the day Rabbit. As there are twenty named days and the beginning of the year is always separated from the last by five days, you can see that there are only four possible names for the year. These are Reed, Flint, House and Rabbit. Look at the picture of the calendar stone on page 68 and you can see the four signs for the year in the inner circle.

Each of these days had thirteen numerals attached to it, 67 so that the name of the year would not just be called Reed, but 1-Reed, or 3-Flint or 7-House and so on. This meant that the year was only called 1-Reed every fifty-two years because 4 × 13 = 52. Fifty-two years was the Mexican equivalent of a century.

In learning about the calendar, you would also learn which days were lucky and which were unlucky, and how they might influence your life. For instance, if you were born on the day 2-Rabbit of any month you would become a drunkard or, if on the day 1-House, you would be destined to be a doctor or midwife. On the first day of the year 1-Reed, you would offer flowers and incense to the god Quetzalcoatl because this was the anniversary of the year in which Quetzalcoatl went away to the east, and it was in a 1-Reed year that he had promised to return.

Aztec calendar stone

As a pupil of the calmecac, you would also learn to paint because the only form of writing was by pictures. You will remember that Montezuma knew that white men had been seen on the coast of the Yucatan. He knew this because letters had been sent to him which described the event, with paintings of the men and of their clothes, and even their ship. These paintings were done on flattened bark which is called 'amatl' paper, and is still used in Mexico today. Maybe you have seen some of these bark paintings of birds and trees.

When you have finished your work at school, you might want to join in the various amusements. As we have imagined that your father is well respected, you might be allowed to join in the hunt. Montezuma was very fond of hunting in the gardens and parks on the mainland. He used to kill birds with a blowpipe. This is a pipe that shoots hard clay balls when you blow it. Another amusement might be to watch or play the ball game that the Mayas also played. Look at the picture (p. 70) of the ball court in the Maya city of Chichen Itza. The game is played in a long court with two walls running down it. In the centre of each wall, quite high up, is a ring and the object of the game is to hit a hard rubber ball through the hoop. It isn't as easy as basket ball or netball because you are not allowed to use your hands. You can hit the ball with your elbows, hips and knees, and you wear padded cotton garments so that the hard ball will not hurt you. It is a very difficult game and goals are not scored very often.

The Mayas also played this game, and there is an interesting sculptured relief in the ball court at Chichen Itza showing a player being ceremonially sacrificed. Scholars think that the greatest honour the captain of the winning team could achieve was to be sacrificed to the gods and so die gloriously. So you can see that it was a very serious game.

Another serious event in your life would be your marriage, which is arranged for you after you leave the calmecac, but first your father will have to ask permission from your teachers to let you leave the school. He would be expected to hold a banquet for your teachers. There would be different kinds of

The ball court at Chichen Itza

meat cooked with a hot sauce of tomatoes and small green peppers (chillies), maize tortillas and cocoa. This would be followed by a pipe of tobacco (the Aztecs had tobacco long before it was known in England). Then your father would formally ask if you might leave the school, and your teacher would formally grant you permission. Perhaps he would also make a short speech, telling you how to behave now that you were going to get married.

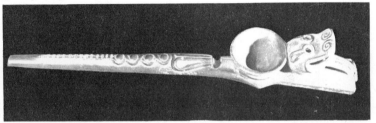

A tobacco pipe

The marriage would then be arranged. Your father would employ a matchmaker – usually an elderly woman – to make all the arrangements. You, yourself, would have very little say in the matter but, as you would hardly ever see girls, you wouldn't know who to choose anyway. Besides, it must be a girl born under a sign favourable to yours, so the priests would be called in to predict who would make a suitable wife. When the girl is chosen and her parents' consent given, the priests are again asked to find a day suitable for the marriage.

This is an important occasion, and all relations and important officials of the district are invited to a feast at the bride's house. After the feast, the bride has a bath and washes her hair and decorates herself with feathers, flowers and the clothes that she has been embroidering for months. Then her family goes with her to her new home. The old woman who has acted as matchmaker carries her over the *threshold*. The marriage ceremony takes place before the shrine in the young man's house. There is singing and dancing and the young couple then go into a small chamber, which might be behind a curtain in 71

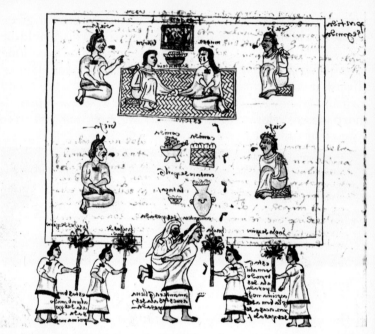

A marriage scene. What is happening in the picture?

the main room, and pray to the gods for four days. On the fifth day there is more feasting and drinking and presents are given.

As a married couple, you would become entitled to certain rights. You could build yourself a small one-roomed house, which would be next door to or near your father's house. Pottery would be given to you (which was made without a wheel). Pots were made out of coils of clay which were built up on top of each other and then smoothed over.

The governor of the district would then allot a piece of land to you, and this was yours so long as you looked after it properly. If you didn't tend the crops, the land would be taken from you and you might become so poor that you would have to sell yourself and your wife as slaves. On the other hand, if you were well off, you would have slaves who looked after the land for you. As it had been predicted that you would become an adviser to the emperor, you would be given tasks to do to help with the running of the district, like keeping count of the number of houses in an area, seeing that farmers and their wives did not wear jewels except on special occasions, or collecting taxes from a group of families.

The Aztecs lived according to strict unchanging rules; the demands of the gods had to be fulfilled; everyone observed the traditions. It is partly because of this rigidity that Montezuma was so frightened when he heard that white men had been seen. He was afraid that all the rules of life would be upset and that the gods in anger would leave the city to its fate.

7 Cortes Lands

We have seen how important the gods were and that the god Quetzalcoatl was particularly feared at the time of our story. He had said: 'I will return in a 1-Reed year and re-establish my rule. It will be a time of great trouble for my people.' But 1415 had been a 1-Reed Year, so had 1467 and Quetzalcoatl had not returned. The next 1-Reed Year was 1519 and the Aztecs were sure that this would be the year in which the god would return. The priests had read signs which foretold that a time of trial was near, and had worked out the exact day on which Quetzalcoatl would arrive. They thought he would come from the east, as this was where the paradise of the sun was. Montezuma was therefore waiting.

Cortes came from the east and landed in 1519 on the very day that had been predicted – Quetzalcoatl's name day! He looked like the traditional picture that the Aztecs had of the god. He had a white face and a black beard; he wore a feathered helmet like Quetzalcoatl's ceremonial head-dress, and he was dressed in black (because it was Good Friday). It was an extra-ordinary piece of luck, as it made the Aztecs feel sure that he was the god, and it is important to understand what it meant if we are to see how Cortes, with his small army of 500 men, was able to conquer Montezuma's vast empire when the king, if he had wanted to, could have raised an army of 150,000 men. In fact, Montezuma had no intention of calling out his army against the god Quetzalcoatl who had returned to claim the land. To resist him would be to risk the god's anger and would bring disaster to the people in the valley of Mexico. It might even lead to a war between Quetzalcoatl and the other gods and this would

The landing of Cortes

mean that the sun, the rain and the wind would forsake the land, and the people would live in darkness. Montezuma also believed that if Cortes was the god, it would, in any case, be impossible to fight against him. He thought his only hope was to welcome Cortes with the richest gifts his kingdom could provide and persuade him to go back to the east where he had come from.

And so, within half an hour of Cortes's landing, two canoes full of Mexican Indians came out to see Cortes and his men. They said their lord Montezuma had sent them to find out who the Spaniards were and what they wanted. They paid Cortes great respect and gave him presents from the emperor – decorated axes, food and some gold ornaments. Cortes gave them some glass beads in return, and offered them some wine. This was a drink unknown to the Aztecs and they carried back favourable reports to their emperor. Cortes told them that they need not feel uneasy as the Spaniards had come to trade.

The Aztecs returned to Montezuma and were very impressed by everything they had seen. Cortes had given them a display of horses, which they had never seen before, galloping at full speed across the sands, and had demonstrated his cannon to them. If they were not extremely frightened, it was certainly very new and strengthened them in the belief that Cortes must be a god.

A week later, Montezuma's messengers returned with more presents. Montezuma had noticed that the conquistadors were particularly interested in the gold objects he had sent when they arrived. He thought that perhaps the god Quetzal-coatl and his followers would be satisfied with rich gifts, just as other gods demanded human sacrifices to satisfy them. Perhaps, he thought, if they got what they wanted, they would go back to where they came from. So he sent his messengers with a hundred slaves and more than thirty loads of gold, silver and ornaments. There was a mask set with precious turquoise stones, silks and coloured robes. The turquoise snake in the picture was one of these first gifts, but the things which most impressed the conquistadors were two circular plates of gold and silver which were as large as carriage wheels. One of them showed the sun and had rich carvings of plants and animals.

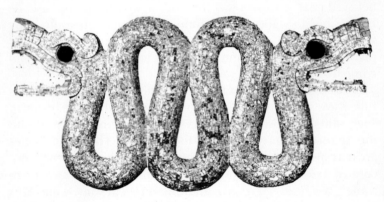

A turquoise snake. It was one of the first presents Montezuma gave to Cortes

Cortes was, of course, extremely surprised. He realised that the Aztecs thought he was a god, but he did not try to make any use of this as he thought the Aztec gods were evil and he was horrified by the sacrifices. He told Montezuma's messengers that he had been sent by *Charles V* of Spain, and was bringing Christianity with him. They did not quite understand who Charles V was, but they must have thought he was a supreme god who ruled over the others.

The fact that Cortes immediately set up the cross of Christianity when he arrived added to the impression that the religion was an important part of the new people's way of life. Cortes, in fact, called the place where he landed 'Villa Rica de la *Vera Cruz*', which means 'the rich town of the true cross'. It is still called Vera Cruz today. He stayed there several months, building a Spanish town. Then Cortes did something very rash. He had all the ships the expedition had sailed in destroyed. Why did he do this? Perhaps he wanted to make escape impossible so that his men would have no alternative but to follow him. Perhaps he wanted to show Montezuma that he intended to come to the capital. The emperor had been friendly so far and Cortes wanted to be invited to the capital. It would save the small army a dangerous journey through an unknown country. Cortes dropped hints to the emperor's messengers, but the invitation never came.

After a time, Cortes realised that Montezuma was not going to be so friendly as to invite visitors, so he sent word to say he was coming. He left behind a *garrison* to guard Vera Cruz, and set out for Mexico-Tenochtitlan. If Cortes had known that Montezuma would not attack him, he could have gone by the most direct route but, of course, it seemed impossible to expect that he would not be attacked. It was a journey of immense daring for so small a group of men to march into what they thought would be a hostile country, but Cortes was an extraordinarily brave man who trusted to luck and believed he could make good use of it. His confidence inspired his army, who went forward in the hope that they would have a share in Montezuma's gold.

Cortes had received help and guides from a small tribe near Vera Cruz who were suffering under Aztec rule. This tribe showed its friendliness by giving eight women as wives to the conquistadors. One of these women proved of great importance to Cortes throughout his journey of conquest. She was called Doña Marina by the Spaniards. Doña Marina spoke Nahuatl, the language of the Mexican Indians, as well as the language of the Mayas. One of Cortes's men spoke the language 77 of the Mayas so that, between the two of them, they were able to translate from Spanish to Nahuatl. Gradually, Doña Marina learnt to speak Spanish herself and so the translating became less clumsy. She was a very intelligent woman, and she helped Cortes greatly in his conversations with Montezuma. She also knew the land, and knew which tribes were friendly towards the Aztecs and which were not.

There were many peoples who suffered under the Aztec rule and who had to send the best of their produce to the capital as taxes. Doña Marina advised Cortes to take his route through states which were dissatisfied with Aztec rule and who might receive him well. But, even if the tribes were friendly, they still had to cross two icy mountain passes, uninhabited desert, stony ravines, rapid rivers and volcanoes.

Cortes was not attacked on his march to the capital until he got to Tlaxcala where he had to fight a fierce battle. This was surprising because the Tlaxcalans were one of the states most hostile to the Aztecs, but Cortes won against amazing odds. The victory added to Montezuma's belief that Cortes was the returning god Quetzalcoatl, and that nothing could stop him.

His fear increased when he received reports that the Tlaxcalans had made friends with Cortes and had offered him an

Cortes's route to Mexico-Tenochtitlan

Cortes and his men fight the Indians

army of 10,000 men. The Tlaxcalans were delighted at this opportunity of fighting against the Aztecs who had invaded their lands for so many years. Cortes, however, refused their help and accepted only a few hundred men to act as guides and porters. He did this because he was beginning to realise that his small force would be powerless against the full Aztec army. His only hope was to pretend that he was on a *mission* of peace so that he would gain an entry into Mexico-Tenochtitlan. He was sure that, once he was there, he could take control of the government and convert the people to Christianity.

It was a risky and courageous thing to do, and the Tlaxcalans thought he was mad not to accept their army. They were also disappointed because they wanted to raid the Aztec capital, but we know that Montezuma had no intention of bringing his

79

army against Cortes. He was supported in this decision by his advisers and the priests. They had read the signs and they agreed with Montezuma about what they meant. They believed that there was nothing they could do except wait for what was bound to happen.

Cortes, of course, did not know this, and did not understand the full importance of the fact that he was mistaken for a god. He acted in such a self-confident way that the Aztecs never doubted he was the god Quetzalcoatl. In the same way, Cortes did not doubt that he had been sent by the God he worshipped to bring the religion of Europe to Mexico. Naturally, he was also interested in the riches and glory of the conquest, but it must have been his sense of mission which gave him such confidence.

So Cortes marched towards Mexico-Tenochtitlan with his small army and a band of Tlaxcalans. They decided to enter the city by the shortest of the three causeways as they were still afraid of attack. Four horsemen rode in front of the procession. Next came the standard bearer, swinging his banner round his head. Foot soldiers followed, their swords sparkling and shields on their shoulders. Behind was a row of riders with lances and

Cortes marches towards the city with his following of Tlaxcalans

swords, and bells tinkling on their bridles. Then came men with cross-bows on their shoulders and quivers full of arrows. Again, riders and many soldiers with coloured plumes of feathers in their helmets. It looked like a colourful procession, but they were very nervous. An army entering along a causeway would have stood little chance against spears flung from thousands of canoes. The Aztecs could easily have destroyed the entire army on the causeway if Montezuma had ordered it, but Montezuma did not. He even sent his nephew and many of the chieftains out of the city to welcome the adventurers on the causeway. They came forward with awe and respect, and kissed the earth in front of Cortes. All the same he was extremely anxious as he suspected that this was a trap to lure the army into the city. Once inside the Aztecs could take up all the bridges along the causeways and the Spaniards would be unable to get out. They knew that if this happened they would become victims for the sacrifices. It was a terrifying thought.

Everything depended on the meeting with Montezuma. When the king himself came out of the city to meet the 'gods', Cortes began to realise that there might be a way in which he could gain control of Montezuma's empire without shedding any blood.

8 Cortes and Montezuma

It must have seemed amazing to the Spaniards that the king of the country they had come to conquer was coming out to meet and receive them as if they had been important royal guests, but such was the case. Montezuma was carried in a *litter* over which was a rich *canopy* of green feathers decorated with gold work, silver, pearls and jade. He was magnificently dressed and wore sandals whose soles were gold and the upper part studded with precious stones. Four chiefs carried the canopy and they, too, were richly dressed. When the procession got near, Cortes dismounted and met Montezuma who had descended from his litter to greet the man he thought was a god. Cortes gave him a necklace of glass 'diamonds' and pearls, and Montezuma presented Cortes with a collar of gold shrimps. The emperor then said: 'Our lord, you are weary. The journey has tired you, but you have arrived on the earth. You have come here to sit on your throne, to sit under its canopy.'

What was Cortes to think when he had this speech translated to him? It must have seemed too good to be true. Either Montezuma was mad or it was a trick. He did not understand that Montezuma was simply treating Cortes with the respect due to the returning god. Montezuma believed that, if he showed the god that he was ruling the country well, he would be satisfied and would go away again.

Cortes and his men were then conducted to the palace of one of the former emperors, which was on the main square in the city. There they were given a fine meal and were entertained well. It looked very friendly but, naturally, they were all very much on their guard. While they were in the city, they never

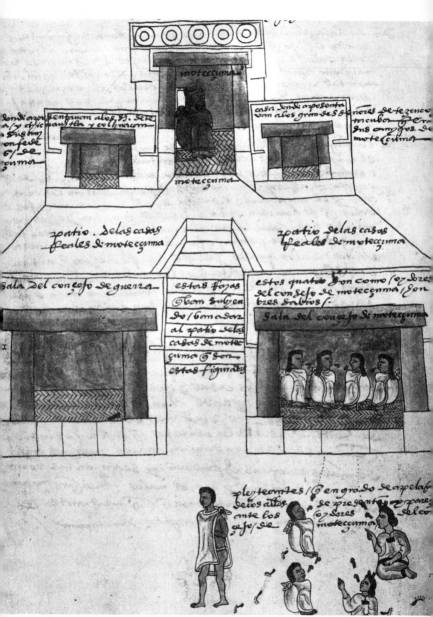

Montezuma's palace. Can you discover the language of the writing?

took off their armour, even for eating and sleeping. They were always alert in case the Aztecs attacked. One of the soldiers got so used to sleeping in his clothes that, in later life, he always slept in this way and wouldn't spend a night in a proper bed.

Cortes now had to do something to make sure he was safe. He had brought his small army into the city unharmed and he had been welcomed in the most extraordinary manner, but he did not feel safe. He had to gain power over the Aztecs. It was obviously hopeless to think of fighting a battle, so Cortes formed a plan of great daring. He would make Montezuma a prisoner and gain power through him. He planned to make the emperor into a puppet king, that is, a person who is king in name but has no power. It had to be done very carefully because, of course, Montezuma, as the powerful head of a great

Cortes talking to Montezuma. Doña Marina is translating

empire, could order the guards to kill the Spaniards if there were any signs of violence.

So Cortes 'invited' Montezuma and his court to come and stay in the palace the Spaniards were living in. He would be made just as comfortable there, and could come and go as he wished, but it would be more convenient if the two leaders could be near each other so that they could discuss matters more easily. Montezuma refused, saying that his advisers would never allow it. Cortes then suggested that Montezuma should tell the court that it was the wish of the gods that he should go and stay with the foreigners. This put Montezuma in a difficult position because he knew it would be humiliating for him to agree to go but, on the other hand, he really did think that a god was commanding it, and did not dare refuse. However, he still tried to avoid doing as Cortes wished by offering to send his son and daughter instead. At this point, one of the captains, frightened that Montezuma would call his bodyguard, shouted out 'stab him if he cries out'. Doña Marina did not translate this but advised the emperor to go with the conquistadors. Finally, Montezuma agreed. There must have been something compelling in Cortes's personality to make Montezuma agree to the demand. Cortes wrote in a letter to the Holy Roman Emperor, Charles V: 'Thus we went to my quarters without causing any commotion in the city, and all was completely as if nothing had happened.'

From then on, Cortes was safe. Montezuma gave in to most of his demands, and Cortes showed the people his power by making Montezuma punish those who were hostile to the Spaniards. On one occasion, he had one of the war commanders, who had attacked the Spanish garrison at Vera Cruz, burnt at the stake and bound Montezuma's feet in chains so that he would not be able to escape and would be forced to watch. The Aztecs were not horrified by death, as their practice of religious sacrifice shows, but this deed was something they had not dreamed of and it shocked them deeply. The sight of their emperor in chains also terrified them, and they began to lose respect for their leader.

After this, Cortes told Montezuma he could go back to the palace if he wanted to, but Montezuma did not dare. He knew that some of the chieftains were in favour of attacking the Spaniards and he felt he was safer where he was.

One of the things Cortes tried to get Montezuma to do was to accept Christianity and so put an end to the practice of human sacrifice that so shocked him. On this point, however, Montezuma was firm. He could not destroy the gods of Mexico because they were more powerful than he, but if Cortes liked, he could set up a cross and a statue of the Virgin near one of the great temples, and he would be given priests to look after them. This was then done and the first mass was sung in the city of the Aztecs. The people who came to watch were impressed by the pomp, but they thought the statue of the Virgin was just another idol. They did not see why they should worship just one idol when they had so many powerful ones of their own. Nevertheless, the Spaniards had made a start in their attempt to convert the Aztecs to Christianity, which was their main excuse for being in the country. You will remember that they thought voyages of conquest were crusades for taking the true religion to barbaric lands. So far, they had not achieved very much, but they had placed the cross on top of a number of pyramids on

A church on top of Cholula pyramid. This is the largest pyramid in Mexico

their way to the capital, and now Montezuma had granted them a shrine within the city. Later, the crosses on top of the old pyramids were to grow into churches.

The other aim of the conquistadors was to make their personal fortunes and seize all the gold and jewels that the country had to offer. Montezuma knew that the soldiers were greedy for gold and not a day passed without his making some present to one of them. He thought they would be satisfied with gold, but the soldiers began to get restless. They had crossed a hostile country and were, so far as they knew, trapped in an island in the middle of a lake. So far they had not got what they came for, and their own expenses had not even been covered. A sealed door had been found in the palace, and they had broken it down to find a hoard of treasure inside. Gold and jewellery worth about £3 million in our money was found there. They sealed up the door again, but tried to work out a way in which they could make the treasure theirs.

Gold jewellery - a warrior's broach

Their scheming proved unnecessary because, when Montezuma heard that his treasure had been found, he decided his wisest course of action would be to give it to the conquistadors since he knew they would take it anyway. They were overwhelmed by his generosity, and immediately set about melting down all the small pieces of gold into ingots. The Spaniards were more interested in solid bars of gold than in intricately worked jewellery. Because of this, a great deal of the Aztec gold craftsmanship has been lost, although it has survived in some parts of the country.

A gold worker melting down gold

Cortes, as head of the expedition, was responsible for the way in which the gold was distributed. He set aside one-fifth for Charles V. He then claimed one-fifth for himself as the representative of Charles; he also claimed for his expenses in Cuba for fitting out the ships, as well as expenses in Mexico. The captains and the priests who were with the expedition also put in heavy claims so that, when the gold which was left was divided among the soldiers, there was no more than the equivalent of £500 each, and this hardly met their own costs (they had been in Mexico over a year). The soldiers were very disappointed and some thought Cortes's behaviour very mean compared with Montezuma's generosity.

Some months after Cortes had established himself in the palace at Mexico-Tenochtitlan and was ruling through Montezuma, ships from Cuba arrived in Vera Cruz. The governor of Cuba had grown suspicious of Cortes and thought he was going to seize all the gold and glory for himself. As you can see from the way Cortes divided the gold, he had forgotten to put aside a share for the governor of Cuba. As the man who had sent out the expedition, at the command of the king, the governor was entitled to some of the spoils. So he sent ships to find out what Cortes was doing, and to fight against him if necessary.

Cortes, therefore, had to go to Vera Cruz, leaving eighty men behind under the command of a man named Alvarado. Cortes had to fight at Vera Cruz and beat his opponent. Most of the soldiers then joined Cortes's expedition, so he gained more men and – most important – more horses. The size of his army was now 1,500 instead of 500, and he was in a much stronger position to march back to Mexico-Tenochtitlan. However, when he got there, he found that things had not been going well in his absence, and his men had been attacked. What had happened was that there had been a religious festival with many sacrifices and much dancing. Alvarado had heard that, after the festival, they intended to attack the Spaniards. Without waiting to find out if this report was true, Alvarado and his men attacked first and fell on the people in the middle of their festival while they were unprepared. The people were very angry and besieged the palace and, but for the intervention of Montezuma, they would certainly have killed all the Spaniards.

This time Cortes walked into the trap that he had feared on first entering the city. Montezuma had stopped bloodshed for the time being but his influence had gone. The warchiefs and priests got together and elected a new ruler, and he was determined not to let a single Spaniard escape alive. He therefore let Cortes march back into the city with his new army, but when they were back in the palace fresh attacks began. Cortes did not know that Montezuma had lost his influence, and thought he could use the emperor again. So he persuaded Montezuma to appear on the balcony and speak to the crowds who were hurling stones, javelins and arrows at the palace. Montezuma replied sadly: 'What more does Malinche want of me? Fate has brought me to such a pass because of him that I do not wish to live or hear his voice again.' Malinche was his name for Cortes. Nevertheless, he dressed himself in his grandest clothes and appeared before his people.

When they saw this grand person whom they had never been allowed to look at, they were awed and paused in their fighting. Montezuma tried to persuade them to cease battle, but they replied that they were now under the command of a new emperor. Some of them must have thought Montezuma was betraying them to the Spaniards because they suddenly started to throw stones again. Three of them hit Montezuma – one on the head. He went in and refused to have his wounds dressed or to see anyone. After three days he died, leaving the Spaniards in a very dangerous position. The man they had ruled through was dead, and the only thing they could do was to escape from the city as best they could.

The soldiers, of course, wanted to take their gold from Montezuma's treasure, but the sensible ones did not take much, as the gold was heavy and weighed them down, making escape difficult. In fact, many of the Spaniards died because of the gold they had taken.

When darkness fell they got ready to make their escape. They decided to leave the city by the shortest causeway. Even this causeway had eight drawbridges in it, and they had all been taken up. The Spaniards therefore built a portable bridge which they planned to carry with them and place over the gaps in the causeway. They left a little before midnight. There was some moonlight but it was raining and so was fairly dark. For a short while they were not observed, but by the time they had reached the causeway and the bridge was being put in place over the first gap the Aztecs were upon them. The trumpets were sounded, and canoes full of men with spears and arrows rowed out to attack them further along the causeway. Only about a third of the army got across the causeway before the portable bridge was destroyed.

Cortes and Doña Marina were among those who escaped and the cannon was saved. Cortes, a commander who always took care of his men, was forced to escape to the sounds of their cries as they were dragged off by the Aztecs, or drowned in the lake but, if he had turned back to rescue them there is little doubt that not one of the army would have escaped alive. Cortes, who had so recently increased the size of his army, now found it reduced again to 500. He himself had been wounded and so had most of his men.

9 The Conquest

After they had crossed to the mainland, the conquistadors were pursued round the lake. They picked up their allies, the Tlaxcalans, who had been camping all this time outside the city, and Cortes's plan was to make for Tlaxcala and seek shelter and aid. Again, he was taking a great risk as the Tlaxcalans might easily turn against him when they saw how things were going with the Aztecs. If the Aztecs conquered, they would punish the Tlaxcalans. If the Spaniards conquered, they would be put in honoured positions and gain wealth and influence. For the moment, the Tlaxcalan allies were friendly. They

The flight to Otumba

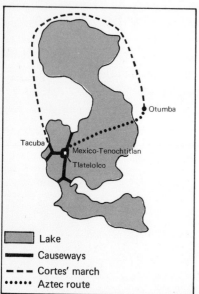

Otumba

Tacuba

Mexico-Tenochtitlan

Tlatelolco

▨ Lake
▬ Causeways
╌ Cortes' march
⋯ Aztec route

marched in front as guides. The wounded walked in the middle and those who were very badly wounded were carried on the horses. The few men who were fit marched at the rear, warding off the arrows and stones of the pursuers. They marched like this for six days, until they got to a place called Otumba.

Meanwhile one of the war chiefs had cut across the lake with a large part of the army and was waiting for Cortes at Otumba.

Cortes spoke to his men and reminded them that at Tlaxcala they had beaten an army just as large, though they were as exhausted then as they were now after their six-day march. He ordered the horsemen to charge and return and then charge again. The Aztecs had never seen fighting like this before. When they had first seen horses, they had been alarmed, but now, with mounted soldiers galloping at them at full speed, they thought they were being attacked by four-legged monsters. Then there were the cannon. Cortes had demonstrated one to Montezuma to show him how powerful they were, but the Aztecs had never faced a cannon in battle. They did not know how to fight against it.

The Aztecs were also at a disadvantage in another way. Their war tactics were not to kill the enemy, but to take prisoners for sacrifice. This was more difficult and it took men away from fighting to guard the prisoners. Since their rise in rank depended on taking prisoners, they were not willing to give them up. Also many of the Aztec soldiers were farmers who had been called away from the fields to give service. It was harvest time and they were not prepared for war.

The result of this battle was victory for Cortes against tremendous odds. He wrote to Charles V:

> They attacked us on all sides so violently that we could not distinguish each other for being so pressed and *entangled* with them. We spent a great part of the day in this struggle until it pleased God that one of these persons, who must have been an important leader, fell and, with his death, the battle ceased.

This victory was very fortunate for Cortes because it strengthened the belief of the chiefs in Tlaxcala that Cortes was likely to conquer the Aztecs and so they decided to give the conquistadors all the help they could. When the army reached Tlaxcala, they were given comfortable accommodation, and women were provided to cook for them. They rested there for a few months until their wounds had healed. Then Cortes ordered his men to build thirteen ships, and the Tlaxcalans helped to cut trees for them. Unless he had ships he could not hope to reach Mexico-Tenochtitlan again. It was too difficult crossing the causeways when the drawbridges had been pulled up, and the Aztecs had thousands of canoes from which they could attack the Spaniards. Cortes knew that his ships would be far superior to the canoes as they were sailing ships and could go much faster. They also could carry more men and, of course, the cannon.

Throughout the expedition of conquest Cortes had one piece of luck after another. He now had another unexpected piece of good fortune. He had used up most of his gunpowder at the battles he had been forced to fight, and there was hardly anything left to feed the cannon. It so happened that a private merchant ship from Spain accidentally put in at Vera Cruz harbour on its way to Cuba. The ship carried gunpowder and arms. Cortes ordered his men at Vera Cruz to buy everything. Some say that he demanded all the gold from his soldiers that had been rescued from Montezuma's gifts in order to pay for the gunpowder. But he needed money in order to carry on the conquest and, if his men gave up their gold, it showed that they still trusted that he could make them rich and that they had confidence in Cortes as a commander.

In Mexico-Tenochtitlan, the Aztecs were also preparing for another battle. They did not have such powerful weapons, and a great deal of work went into making them. We saw that they fought with stones, arrows and javelins, but they had no metal weapons. Their arrow heads were made from a hard stone called obsidian. This is a black stone, sometimes used in jewellery today. The arrow makers had to use sharp razors of the obsidian stone to make arrow heads, and it took a long time to prepare the vast number that was needed.

Things were turning out well for Cortes, but the Aztecs were not so fortunate. One of the men Cortes had brought back with him from Vera Cruz was a Negro servant, and he had smallpox. Smallpox was not known to the Aztecs and so their bodies had not built up any resistance to it, whereas the Spaniards had. This man was left behind when the Spaniards fled, and an epidemic spread throughout the city, killing off a great many of the Aztec warriors, including the new emperor, who had only reigned a few months. The chiefs then met again, and chose the bravest man in the royal family to be their leader for the fight they knew was coming. This was *Guatemoc*, a young man of twenty-five, and he was to be the last emperor of the Aztecs. His name means 'Falling Eagle'.

Guatemoc got together a vast army by summoning warriors

Guatemoc

95

from the nearest tax-paying tribes. Each of these armies had its own commander, and the war chiefs did not always agree among themselves on how the war should be fought. Some of them were hostile to the Aztecs in any case, and fought in rather a half-hearted fashion because they hoped the Spaniards would win.

Cortes then undertook to do what no other army had ever attempted – to storm Mexico-Tenochtitlan. The city was so well fortified that none of the tribes hostile to the Aztec empire had ever dared to attack it, but Cortes had ships; he had superior fighting men, stronger weapons, and his belief that God was on his side. He inspired his men in this belief, and they went forward to what was to be a long and bitter siege. For over two months the men suffered from lack of food, disease, little sleep, and fierce attacks by day and by night. The soldier Bernal Diaz wrote: 'Wounded and bandaged with rags, we had to fight from morning till night for, if the wounded had not fought but stayed behind in camp, there would not have been twenty sound men in each company to go out.'

Cortes divided his army into three sections, and each section advanced up one of the causeways, step by step, while Cortes himself commanded the thirteen ships and gained mastery over the lake. The armies could advance only very slowly because they had to ward off a rain of arrows from the Aztecs fighting from their canoes and from the flat-topped roofs of the houses. One of the first things the Spaniards achieved was to cut off food and water supplies from the mainland to the city. It was not so easy to prevent food getting through, as the Aztecs could dodge the ships in their canoes, but there was an aqueduct along one of the causeways which brought fresh water into the city. Cortes had this destroyed, and the Aztecs found it very difficult to get drinking water. In fact, towards the end of the battle, they were drinking from polluted wells in the city, and so were weakened by all kinds of diseases. This may have been why Guatemoc eventually had to surrender.

He had tried one plan after another, and had even tried to trick the three sections of the Spanish army into thinking that

Cortes and his men advance along the causeway
Cortes receives the surrender of the last Aztec King

Cortes was dead, but he was not able to resist the strong fighting and good leadership of the Spaniards. When they had captured all three causeways and had met in the great market square of Tlateloco, burning all houses on their way, Guatemoc finally surrendered. This was on 13 August 1521, two years after Cortes had landed in Mexico. Guatemoc tried to escape across the lake, but was captured by Cortes's men. After seventy-five days the fighting suddenly stopped and there was silence again. There had been shouting, drums, trumpets, whistles and cannon fire for so long that when the noise stopped some of the soldiers thought they had gone deaf.

Cortes at last re-entered the city and claimed Mexico as a dominion of Spain. One of the first things he did was to look for the gold they had been forced to leave behind. He tortured Guatemoc to find out where it was. Guatemoc was then taken as a prisoner, and went with Cortes on an expedition to conquer the area which is now Guatemala (named after the emperor). There he was hanged.

So ended the Aztec empire.

After the conquest, an Aztec poet wrote this poem (Tlatelolco is the market square where the Aztecs finally surrendered):

Our cries of grief rise up
And our tears rain down,
For Tlatelolco is lost.
The Aztecs are fleeing across the lake;
They are running away like women.

How can we save our homes, my people?
The Aztecs are deserting the city;
The city is in flames, and all
Is darkness and destruction.

Weep, my people;
Know that with these disasters
we have lost the Mexican nation.
The water has turned bitter,
Our food is bitter!
These are the acts of the Giver of Life.

10 After the Conquest

The first task of the Spaniards was to clear up the city, which was in ruins after the fighting. Houses had been burned and temples had been pulled down to make barricades. The Spaniards destroyed all the temples, as they thought them evil places. With the stone they built Christian churches, and a Spanish town gradually grew up. The Aztecs who had fled returned to occupy the city, and were forced to change their religion to Christianity, and receive new names. Franciscan and Dominican friars came over from Spain as missionaries to convert the Mexican Indians, but they did not really understand the meaning of Christianity. As far as they could see, their old gods had deceived them and a new god was being offered. They accepted the new god in the hope of a better life. They also liked the mass and the religious ceremonies because they had been used to ceremony in their own religion, but they found it difficult to accept the idea that there was only one god and, on the whole, Christ and the Virgin became idols which were added to their family shrines. In Mexico today idols are still worshipped in some remote parts of the country and, even in places where they do not really believe the idols are gods, they still *superstitiously* leave corn gods in the fields to encourage the growth of crops.

The Christian missionaries thought they would never be able to make the Mexican Indians understand the 'true religion' and began to treat them as inferior people because of this, but then one day, ten years after the conquest, a vision appeared to a Mexican Indian peasant. The peasant said a vision of the Virgin Mary had appeared to him in his home town of Guadalupe, and she had ordered that a church should be built on that spot.   99

The church at Guadalupe today. It was built on the spot where the peasant saw the miracle
The santuary at Ocotlan today

To prove his story, he showed the Spanish missionary to whom he spoke his handkerchief, which had a picture of the Virgin printed on it. The peasant said that she had left it for him. The Mexican Indians marvelled at this story, and a church was built on the spot, which you can see in the picture opposite. In a very short time, churches were being built all over the country; there are still about 10,000 churches of this period in Mexico today. The church in the bottom picture has a gold interior made by a Mexican Indian peasant. He devoted twenty-seven years of his life to the work.

The Catholic missionaries gave the Aztecs an education. They set up church schools and taught Spanish and religion. They also brought European inventions. The Mexican Indians learned how to use the wheel. Just think how many ways you can use wheels when at work in town or country; making pots on a wheel is only one of them. Of course the churchmen who showed them these new ways gained a lot of power over the Mexican Indians. Unfortunately, they did not always use power to help the people. The Spanish settlers who were given land to cultivate were allowed to demand a certain amount of work in their fields from a Mexican Indian peasant. In return, the Spaniards protected the peasants and looked after their religious education. This was called the 'encomienda' system. Whether they had been rich or poor before, all Mexican Indians were now forced to work as slaves. They were worse off than Aztec slaves had been, for the Aztecs had treated their slaves rather better. The Spaniards stood over them with whips to see that they did the work properly, and they were rarely given justice. The Tlaxcalans did not suffer so much as they had been allies of the Spaniards, but they still had to agree to being ruled.

This was a sad change from the days when Cortes set out to bring Christianity to Mexico. The reason was that the men who came to Mexico after the conquest just wanted to make as much money as they could and then return to Spain to live the rest of their lives in leisure on a rich estate. They were often ruthless men who were anxious not to allow the natives of the country to become more powerful than themselves. Charles V and later

A modern painting by Diego Rivera shows Spanish treatment of Mexican Indians

kings tried to get fair play for the Mexican Indians but Spain was so far away from Mexico that this was very difficult. After 1588 communication between the two countries was especially difficult because England had destroyed the Spanish Armada, and Spanish ships were never safe from attack. We must remember, then, that the Spanish kings did not intend the Mexican Indians to be treated cruelly. This happened because of greedy adventurers who were only interested in making themselves rich. In recent times, Mexican painters have done large wall-paintings to show how these adventurers treated the Indians. Look at the painting by Diego Rivera opposite, which shows Cortes in a very bad light. He looks like an ugly, evil hunchback – not at all the powerful and dominating man that the soldiers in the expedition thought he was.

Diego Rivera's painting of Cortes

Cortes became quite a powerful figure after the conquest, though it took over a year before the king of Spain made his appointment as Captain-General of Mexico official. Meanwhile he surrounded himself with a court fit for a very magnificent lord. He had a large household, and even when he went on a fresh campaign to subdue the provinces of Mexico he took with him a dinner service of gold and silver plate, three priests, a butler, a steward, and other personal servants. He also had five musicians, an acrobat, and a puppet master to amuse his company. Later, Cortes was made marquess of the rich and fertile valley of Oaxaca, but a Spanish lord was appointed as Governor of Mexico. This was a great disappointment to Cortes, who felt that he had a much better right than any other man to rule Mexico, and also that he knew the country and the people best. In fact, Cortes did not gain any position of great honour as a result of conquering Mexico for Spain.

In 1535 Pizarro conquered Peru, which had far more gold treasure to offer than Mexico. Cortes's brave deeds no longer interested the Court of Spain; he was not given command of another expedition, and was treated by everyone as an old soldier whose great moment was in the past.

Very few of the other conquistadors made their fortunes either. The captains in Cortes's small army were sent off to subdue other tribes in Mexico, and many of them suffered far worse hardships than they had during the capture of Mexico-Tenochtitlan. Many of the soldiers were in debt to one another. They might owe each other money for a sword they had borrowed, and doctors' fees were very high. Even with the land and slaves they were given, it could take two years before they had paid all their bills. The soldier, Bernal Diaz, who has been quoted before in this book, said: 'I have gained no wealth to leave my children and descendants, except this true story, which is a remarkable one!' To us, today, this 'true story' is worth more than any piece of Mexican gold.

The one person who did do well out of the conquest was Doña Marina. She was married to a Spanish captain and had a town house and a country house, and a garden that had belonged to Montezuma. After her death she was worshipped as a mountain goddess, and the mountain called La Malinche, near Tlaxcala, is named after her.

The more honoured conquistadors and noblemen who came out to live in Mexico after the conquest were granted lands and they lived on large estates called 'haciendas'. The Mexican Indians had to work on these estates. Sometimes, they even had 104 to work on land that had once belonged to them. Most of the farmers were allowed to keep the land that they had at the time of the conquest, and this plot of land was then kept in the family. As the family grew larger, the plot of land did not give enough crops to supply the family's needs. Under the Aztecs, a man who got married was given a plot of land which went back to the state when he died, and the governor of the district looked after the communal land, and divided it among the people when necessary, but the Spaniards did not realise this, and they allowed the governors to keep the land they had under their care. It then became an estate which was handed down from father to son, and so a new nobility was formed, dividing the people into two classes – the rich and the poor. Before the arrival of the Spaniards, wealth had not meant a man would be respected. As we saw in chapter 5, you would be honoured for your achievements, not your riches.

The Spaniards married Mexican Indians and the children of these mixed marriages are called *mestizos*. Most Mexicans today are mestizos. Cortes made it a law that all men should marry either before they came out to Mexico or within a few months of arrival. His own wife came from Cuba to join him, but died soon after. The idea was that mixed marriages would help the Spaniards and Mexicans to understand each other, so that they would be able to live together in peace, but this never really happened. In Mexico today pure-blooded Spaniards are disliked by mestizos, and cannot rise to important government positions. Mestizos prefer to use the old Indian names that were in their families before the conquest, rather than the Spanish names they were given.

Although the Spaniards were very unpopular there was no rebellion until the nineteenth century. Then, in 1810, a Spanish priest called Padre Miguel Hidalgo spoke to the people in his parish encouraging them to demand equality and more land. His speech came to be known as the 'grito de dolores', which means 'the cry from the people of Dolores'. Hidalgo was later shot by the Spaniards, but his words encouraged the peasants to rise against Spanish rule. A man named Madero led the rebellion, and he became the first leader of independent Mexico.

However, the large haciendas, owned by one rich man, still existed and the gap between rich and poor was very wide. A hundred years after Mexico had freed itself from Spanish rule there was another revolution which tried to give equal opportunities to the rich and the poor. This was in 1910. The haciendas were all split up and the land was divided among the people. Mexico became a republic, which it still is. The party which rules Mexico is called the Institutional Revolutionary Party, and the name of the president, at the moment of writing this book, is Luis Echeverria.

This is the strange story of how a rich and powerful people was conquered by a handful of bold men. These conquistadors arrived – though they did not know it – with a special magic, which gave them their first victories. Treated as gods by the Aztecs, they fought in the name of the one God, doing brave and terrible things; but, when they had conquered triumphantly, greed for gold became more important than religion or anything else. The people whose country they had taken were trodden under their feet. It is an exciting story, but a very tragic one.

How Do We Know?

When you read a history book, you are probably always asking yourself 'How do we know this happened? How do we know he said that?' Fortunately, the conquest of Mexico was so famous an adventure that a number of people who were there wrote about this exciting happening. Cortes, himself, wrote five letters to Charles V, telling him the story of the conquest. The soldier, Bernal Diaz, who has been quoted several times, wrote a history of the conquest of Mexico when he was an old man looking back on the adventures of his youth. After the conquest, missionaries came out and spoke to the Indians and reconstructed histories in that way.

But histories written by the Spaniards might only see stories from their side, so we have to look at original Indian accounts as well. There are not many of these because the Aztecs had no writing of their own. In order to write down their memories, they had first to learn the Latin alphabet, and then they used it to write the sounds of their own language. In this way, some Songs of Conquest have come down to us (one is quoted at the end of chapter 9), but most of the Indian history is in pictures which tell the story of the conquest, and many of these have been used to illustrate this book. They are not always easy to understand, but, when you have looked at a few of them, you will see that they describe the scene far better than words can.

Things to Do

1. Make a scrap book of explorations today. You could include space travel, journeys to the Poles, undersea adventures, mountaineering and travel in remote parts of Africa and South America.
2. Find and read the picture book 'The Life and Times of Cortes' published by Paul Hamlyn. Your local library may have it.
3. Early Mexico was not influenced by other peoples. How has modern Britain been affected by other countries such as the United States of America?
4. Imagine you have been asked to design a new symbol for the Republic of Mexico. Use the eagle, serpent and cactus to make a design.
5. If you had lived in Spain when the New World was being discovered, would you have joined an expedition? Give reasons.
6. What do you think of the Aztec religious practice of human sacrifice? Do you think the Spaniards were right to change the religion?
7. Get a map of Mexico from the Mexican Tourist Office. The ruins of ancient pyramids are marked on it. Draw a circle round each one. How many are there?
8. Re-read the description on pages 59–60 and make a painting of chieftains in the presence of Montezuma.
9. Write a play about Montezuma and Cortes.
10. How many countries can you think of that had slaves at one time in their history? What do you think life as a slave would have been like?
11. If you had been an Aztec, do you think you would have believed that Cortes was a god?
12. Mexico has been in the news recently because the Olympics and the World Cup Finals were held there. Sportsmen coming to Mexico have to stay a while to get used to the climate. Do you know why?

Glossary

astrologer, one who made forecasts from studying the stars

Bering Straits, the narrow stretch of water between the continents of Asia and America

canopy, cloth covering held over throne

cassava bread, bread which keeps for a long time made from the root of a plant

causeway, raised roadway across the lake connecting city to mainland

Charles V, Holy Roman Emperor and king of Spain

civilisation, educated way of life

cog-wheel, a wheel with a toothed rim which can turn another toothed wheel

composure, calmness

cultivated, grown by farming the land

to dedicate, to give oneself fully to a single purpose, e.g. religion

empire, a collection of states or countries which were originally independent, under the rule of one of those states or countries

to entangle, to tangle together, make into a muddle

fallow, land left without any crops for a year so that it becomes fertile again

to focus, to fix the eyes (or a camera lens) on an object

garrison, soldiers stationed in a fort

geniality, cheerfulness

guileless, without cunning

hereditary, passed down from father to son (or nearest relative)

hieroglyphs, little drawings used for each syllable or letter in picture-writing

Hispaniola, the first Spanish settlement in the West Indies, now Haiti and the Dominican Republic

hoist, lift up

jackal, a kind of wild dog

jade, a very hard green or green and white precious stone. The Aztecs valued it highly.

litter, a chair or royal throne in which an important person is carried

maize, cereal crop, known in England as sweet corn and corn on the cob

mammoth, elephant of a kind that no longer exists

Michelangelo (1475–1564), famous Italian sculptor and painter

mission, a journey with a purpose, often religious.

mosaic, decoration made up of little pieces of glass, stone, coloured paper, feathers and so on

nomadic, wandering from place to place

obeisance, bow

observatory, building for looking at the stars and planets

omen, sign foretelling an event

predictions, things foretold

proclamation, notice or instruction given to the public

to re-establish, to bring back

to sacrifice, to offer something (or person) to a god; a *sacrifice* is the thing or person offered

shrine, altar or tomb which has religious idols or objects

superstitious, believing things that are not supported by fact and are often unreasonable

threshold, doorstep or other point of entry to a house

tribute, tax paid in the form of goods or money by subdued nation to its emperor

Vera Cruz; the landing place of Cortes, now Mexico's main port

Yucatan peninsula, low peninsula to east of Mexico-Tenochtitlan where Mayas lived. Consists of Yucatan, Quintana Roo, Guatemala and British Honduras

A

We ... copyright
ma ...
Bea ... *he Broken*
Spe ... from *The*
Con ... . Cohen,
196 ...

For ... the
foll ...

Page
  6
 11
 13
 16
 17
 18

 20
 21
 22
 23
 26

 27
 28
 29
 30
 32
 33
 34
 36 B ... al
 40 I.
 41 I.
 42 I.
 43 I.
 45 S ...
 46 M ...   102 I.N.A.H.
 47 Scala   103 I.N.A.H.